INDIVIDUALIZED INSTRUCTION:
Every Child a Winner

INDIVIDUALIZED INSTRUCTION:
Every Child a Winner

GERTRUDE NOAR

John Wiley & Sons, Inc.
New York • London • Sydney • Toronto

Library of Congress Catalogue Card Number: 71-179420

ISBN 0-471-64156-1 (cloth)
ISBN 0-471-64157-x (paper)

Printed in the United States of America.

10 9 8 7 6 5 4 3

FOREWORD

"Someday after mastering the winds,
the waves, the tides and gravity,
We shall harness for God
the energies of Love,
And for the second time in history
Man will discover fire."

These words of Teilhard de Chardin capture as well as any I know the spirit of Gertrude Noar's book. And, the spirit behind the practical advice and how-to-do ideas is what has made so effective and powerful the work and writing of Gertrude Noar over the past two decades. One important difference between this book and others which are highly critical of schools is that the author knows and cares about both children and teachers. She listens to both. She loves both.

Because she cares and loves, she goes far beyond exhortation and inspiration to provide detailed, specific suggestions about what to do. The book is specifically for teachers, teacher aides, and others who work with children in schools. It is designed specifically to help teachers who work with those youngsters the educational system is failing most—children who are poor, handicapped, alienated, children who are "different" because of their color, their religion, their race.

My interest in this kind of book rests on my belief that providing these children with better education depends on helping teachers develop new skills, new knowledge, and more positive attitudes toward children. Nothing else can do it. So, "preservice and inservice teacher training" (an unpretty and jargony label if there ever was one) is at the core of the problem of school improvement.

This book, illumined by a compassionate spirit and rich with specificity, can be an important part of the "professional development" of anyone who is working in the schools and who wants the schools to serve all children more adequately.

Don Davies
Associate Commissioner
Bureau of Educational Personnel Development
U.S. Office of Education

PREFACE

It has been my privilege for the past twenty years to meet with many groups of public school teachers and administrators in all parts of the nation and to sit often in classrooms to watch the teachers at work with children and teen-agers. These meetings were inservice education activities which school superintendents and directors of instruction hoped would bring about improvement in classroom instruction. For some years, initiated and supported by community agencies, these efforts were directed toward creating more positive attitudes toward racial and religious minority group children.

Many programs during the last five years were, and still are, specifically for teachers facing desegregation of schools or already teaching across race lines. Inservice education programs of this nature, especially in the South, would not have been held, nor could they have been financed, without the support of the federal government under the Civil Rights Act of 1964. Essential to this work has been the establishment of Consultative Centers for Human Relations and Desegregation. In the Oklahoma, North Carolina, and Arkansas centers with which I have worked intensively, directors and staff members have worked with great dedication and commitment to sensitize boards of education to teachers' needs for help, to stimulate, encourage, and help them formulate desegregation plans, and to assist superintendents in developing proposals for inservice education programs.

The movement to eliminate poverty focused nationwide attention on the children of the urban and rural slums and ghettos. People became irate over the failure of the public schools to provide full and equal opportunities for all children to realize their potentials. Inservice education activities began to devote most of their time to the psychological and sociological damages suffered by children whom grinding poverty caused to be severely handicapped when they entered public school. These programs, too, were encouraged and supported by the Department of Health, Education and Welfare, Office of Education, under the Elementary and Secondary Education Act.

The underlying purpose of the nationwide inservice and preservice education movement remains the improvement of classroom instruction. Teachers have gone voluntarily and without extra compensation, or only a small stipend, to winter and summer institutes and workshops where they have engaged in interracial confrontations and have been talked to and with about social issues and problems, about intergroup attitudes, about theories and philosophies of education, about the causes of behavior problems, and about the nature of learning disabilities. Thousands of articles and hundreds of books have been written for them. Now they are saying, "Yes, we understand all that, but we still don't know what to do. Tell us how to do it. *How do you teach individual children in a class of thirty or more who are far below grade level while others are far above? What do you do when they can't read? How do you turn them on?*"

The answers teachers are looking for are not all known. Those we do know are many and complex. Moreover, answers, if they are to effect change, must be personalized after having observed the individual teacher as he works with children or teen-agers. However, after having done just that and then having listened to their specific questions, I found some answers which, when simplified, made specific, and illustrated with true stories, provide teachers and teachers-to-be with ideas about ways to change their methods of instruction so that more children will learn more, about more, more easily. These are the methods I have described in this book.

I must acknowledge with thanks the teachers and children in

schools in North Carolina, Arkansas, and Oklahoma who have allowed me to visit their classrooms to watch them at work. Directors of the Centers, especially Marion Bird in Raleigh and A. B. Wetherington in Arkadelphia, Arkansas; College professors in Western Kentucky University, O. L. Gladman and James Hicks; Mrs. Juanita Sandford of Henderson College, Arkadelphia; consultants in workshops and institutes and classroom teachers (all of whom, having read the manuscript, urged me to make it available to teachers) have been most helpful.

This book has been developed to answer the following questions that teachers ask (page xi) and is based on the educational principles included in those questions.

Gertrude Noar

QUESTIONS TEACHERS ASK

How can I reach "all children"? I have too many and I'm only human. I can't *love* everybody.

How can I "teach human relations" and the curriculum, the course of study, too?

Is it possible to give every child a success experience every day?

All that students and parents care about is marks. Why are students not interested in learning?

What should I do when a child refuses to obey me?

Isn't it necessary to paddle some children?

I can't control some children. Why? What shall I do about it?

How do I turn them on?

If I use able children to help others, won't they be missing out?

The slow ones resent being helped by bright ones. What do I do about that?

Some children just aren't ready for school. They don't even understand what I say. How can I teach them? What do they need most?

I can't get teaching machines and reading machines. I don't even have enough books. How can I change the curriculum and my methods?

I'm in a secondary school. I have 150 pupils every day. Of course I lecture and I have a textbook I am supposed to cover. What can I do about students who can't read the book?

What can I do about those who can't keep up? If I give them too much time, am I not harming those who do want to learn? What about our standards? What about high ability pupils?

Does individualized instruction mean I have to teach each pupil by himself? What can I do about pupils who don't know their fundamentals? Can I teach them and still get others ready for college? How can I teach individuals when I have 150 a day?

What about grouping by ability?

What do you mean by learning styles?

What can we do about marks and report cards? Will parents let us do without marks? Don't colleges demand marks for students?

Without competition how will a student know what his real level of ability is? What will happen to standards? Competition runs the country; he has to learn how or fail in life.

Basic Principles of Education

Every child grows. What happens to him in school as he tries to establish relationships may either hinder or facilitate his growth. Acceptance must replace rejection; success must replace failure.

Individuals differ in brain power and development, in the rate of learning, and in the methods of learning, yet each one is of supreme worth as a human being.

Success in learning frees the energy needed to make an effort and together with praise provides profound motivation. Failure defeats, crushes, inhibits learning.

Everyone behaves as he perceives himself to be. Experiences in school convince some pupils that they are inferior. A negative image of self produces behavior inimical to learning. The school's responsibility is to build positive self concepts—feelings of worth, self-confidence, self-respect.

Behavior is caused. The teacher must seek the causes of unproductive and disruptive behavior. Punishment unrelated to causes is usually ineffective as a deterrent or corrective measure.

Language learning for economically disadvantaged children is facilitated by direct sensory experiences.

Mass instruction is the least effective method of instruction because pupils differ widely in readiness, potentiality, levels of development, skills, and learning styles.

Individualized instruction can begin with the mass but moves toward the individual through subgroups.

Learning to learn is more important and enduring than learning facts. Nonparticipating children usually do not know what they must do in order to learn. Every child should become an independent learner at whatever level his native endowment permits.

G. N.

CONTENTS

p. 43-44

INDIVIDUALIZED INSTRUCTION:
Every Child a Winner

1 BASIC HUMAN NEEDS

"If we would prepare youth properly for the human world they must live in and for the human problems they must solve, the curriculum of our schools must provide students opportunities to explore human questions. Vital questions of values, beliefs, feelings, emotions, and human inter-relationships in all forms must be integral parts of the curriculum.

"It is a fascinating thing that the human qualities of love, compassion, concern, caring, responsibility, honor, indignation and the like are largely left to accident in our schools."

Arthur W. Combs
"An Educational Imperative: The Human Dimension"
ASCD Year Book, 1970

Basic Human Needs

Human beings at all stages of life need satisfaction of certain deep-seated emotional needs. Although these needs are common to all children, satisfaction or deprivation of satisfaction becomes an entirely individual matter rooted in personal life experience at home, in society, and in school. The individual child, as well as the school group to which he belongs, is damaged if his own deep-seated needs are not met in his home and community and school. Although the home and society play a large part in meeting these needs, the teacher can do little about that. What he can and must do for each and every child in the school is what individualization of instruction is all about.

When an individual child's needs are not satisfied, his physical well-being may be affected. (Some children wilt for no other discernable cause.) A child's mental growth is likely to slow up. (Some normal children seem to be retarded or they do not learn how to read.) A child's emotional health is bound to be poor. (Some have temper tantrums, others suffer from depression and become silent, and still others commit suicide.)

Two kinds of emotional needs are especially relevant to instruction in the classroom. One is the need for acceptance. The other is the need to achieve. Every child must believe that his teacher accepts him, likes him, wants him in the room, that he

1

belongs there no matter how different from other pupils he may be. If he feels rejected and excluded, his learning as well as his social behavior will reflect it. The teacher who is concerned about a child's progress or lack of involvement in learning must examine his own relationship with that child to determine whether he communicates acceptance or rejection.

Words, the tone of voice, its volume and inflection are verbal signals which tell a pupil that he is accepted. When a teacher yells, "Get out!" the pupil knows without doubt that he is rejected. Unfortunately, teachers find it easier to tell children that they are not liked than to say "I like you." Mrs. Greene, a junior high school teacher, was having trouble with one of her classes. She brought the matter to her consultant who asked, "Do you like them? Have you told them so?" "Come to think of it," the teacher replied, "I believe they think I hate them." The next day, before the class departed, Mrs. Greene said to them, "I want to tell you something before you go. We have been having a rough time together. It has been hard on all of us, me too, but I want you to know that I like you very much and I look forward to your return tomorrow so we can make a fresh start." The pupils sat in silence for a moment—they seemed stunned. Then one of them spoke up, "Mrs. Greene, you like us? How can you? We're so horrible!"

Rejection and acceptance contribute to the individual's feelings about himself, and he behaves as he perceives himself to be. A child who feels unliked believes there is something wrong with him that makes people reject him. How then can he like himself? And if he does not like himself, he cannot like anyone else. He is already licked so what's the use of trying. These thoughts and feelings create anxiety which, in addition to his negative self-image, block learning. The teacher must, therefore, ask himself, "What am I doing to convince the individual child, about whom I am worried, that I do accept him and like him and want him in my room? What am I doing? What am I doing too much? What must I stop doing, begin to do, do more or less of, and where do I begin tomorrow morning?"

Nonverbal signals of rejection are as important as words and voice. A shrug, a sweep of the arm that says come to me or stay away, a sneer or curl of the lip, raised eyebrows, a frown, a smile, contact convey their positive and negative messages. A school principal, trying to convince a child that his teacher liked him, was taken aback when the boy replied, "Well, if she does, tell her to tell her face."

Contact is especially important in developing warm, accepting relations. Any touch that is not reassuring, that does not convey security and trust, should be avoided. This means that teachers ought not to slap, push, shove, punch, or whip pupils. Some teachers are reluctant to give up the idea that they can do without whipping children. They tend to believe that the children they want to whip are punished that way at home and will respond to nothing less. The teacher, however, is not the parent and should not try to act like one. Therefore, he can say to a child in need of correction, "I am not going to hit you. I am not your father or your mother, I am your teacher, and I do not intend to strike you because I respect you too much. I respect you as a human being and intend to treat you like one. If you were an animal and could not think and talk, I might have to hit you to make you behave. You are not an animal, you are a person. You have a mind and you must use it. Come let us reason together. I will not paddle you but I will not let you continue to misbehave. If you cannot change your behavior you cannot stay with us. Now let us talk and then *you make the decision*."

Self-respect is of the utmost importance to every human being. It comes to the child as a result of being treated with respect. If he does not experience such treatment, especially from those who are significant to him, he comes to believe that he is unworthy of respect, so there is no use for him to try to act in a respectable manner. Every person behaves the way he sees himself to be.

In addition to finding acceptance in life, every human being, especially as he is growing up, must have experiences in which he achieves, accomplishes, is successful. The rest of this book is devoted to ways by which classroom teachers can more fully meet these basic needs common to all children at all age levels.

2 BEHAVIOR—DISCIPLINE

"Two modern principles of behavior:
  1—People behave according to how things seem to them.
  2—The most important ideas any of us have are those ideas about ourselves."

Arthur W. Combs
"Seeing Is Behaving" an address presented at ASCD in Seattle

Behavior—Teachers Call It Discipline

Many teachers are more concerned about behavior in the classroom than about learning. They say, "If only they'll behave, I can teach them. What's the matter with them today? Tell us what to do."

All behavior is caused. Before dealing with actions the teacher must know something about the nature of behavior and search for the reasons why a child or teen-ager acts in a specific way at a particular time. The following review of some general principles should help.

The individual most frequently behaves as he sees or imagines himself to be. His actions also depend upon his ability to see alternatives, to think about them critically, and to make choices in terms of the consequences he envisions. Both emotional maturity and intellectual development play their respective roles. However, unless the child knows something about alternatives, he cannot choose between them. This is one reason for believing that a classroom in which both lower and middle class pupils live and work together is a good place for children to learn about behavior, especially about the behavior necessary to achieve social mobility. Lower class children need to see how middle class children act before they can decide whether they want to act the same way.

Children who have been unsuccessful in school or who have suffered rejection by peers and teachers or who may be treated as "the underdog" at home often fantasize themselves as leaders, as "big shots," and may, in their daydreams, see themselves beating up other children or destroying someone they deem of lesser worth than themselves. If occasion arises such a child may act out his fantasy in violence against a classmate or school property.

Some people are highly suggestible. The tales of violence spread across the daily press and broadcast on television every day give them ideas which they proceed to act out. It is easy for militant leaders who are convinced that violence is the only way to change what they do not like about schools to arouse suggestible junior and senior high school students who may be eager to follow the lead of such a role model.

Feelings of guilt need to be alleviated. A scapegoat provides relief from guilt feelings. Sometimes sex activities and urges not understood by the child plague him with guilt. Defiance and disobedience at home produce regret and guilt for some children in early adolescence. Failure at school makes some ashamed especially if parents use their children's success for social status purposes. When feelings of guilt mount, the accompanying anxiety level may become unendurable. Then the child, to get relief, commits an act that he knows will bring him punishment. He may destroy something or steal. He makes little effort to conceal whatever he does. Punishment will help him for the time being but will make no permanent change in his behavior.

Excessive anxiety that the individual cannot control or channel or reduce may be the cause of compulsive behavior so much of which disrupts classrooms today. Such a child passing by the school on the weekend and feeling dislike for it because he fails there may impulsively pick up a brick and throw it at the window. If his impulse is to hurt because he has been hurt, he may direct it against a person whom he has heard his parents blame for what is wrong in the neighborhood.

Not all impulsive behavior in the classroom can be attributed to anxiety. Pupils who impulsively get up and run around, who toss wads of paper in the midst of a lesson, who answer back,

who argue with the teacher, who make sudden lunges at classmates, who yell across the room to friends whenever they feel
like it are children who do not know how to cope with themselves. The reasons for their behavior and its consequences are
rarely discussed by a class so they do not know that it contributes
to what hurts them most, namely rejection by their teacher and
their peers. Personal feelings and emotions should be discussed
until children understand what causes them and how and why
to control them. The limits to behavior must be set by the
group.

As soon as a teacher meets a group of children or teen-agers, he
must establish himself as the teacher. He is not the parent; he
is not the pal. He is the teacher and as such has specific responsibilities and objectives which he needs to spell out for his pupils.
He must convince them that he has no intention of abdicating
his role. But just as he tells the students about his role, he must
give them full opportunity to identify their responsibilities and
their objectives. Above all there must be agreement that the
one objective they all have in common is learning. This process
of finding common problems, of setting up common objectives,
and of determining how to reach common goals makes a group
out of individuals. Furthermore, it establishes a climate within
which all can live.

When objectives are clearly defined, the next step is to describe
and to discuss the kind of behavior that gets in the way and the
kind of behavior that helps all to reach their goals. Rarely will
individuals behave in ways that the peer group does not like.
Some will test the teacher and/or the group to find out if they
mean what they say. Testing behavior cannot be ignored but
must be dealt with at once. The most effective corrective measure
is to put the offender out of the group; for that is what he wants
least. This should be a temporary exclusion. Whenever a pupil
is put out his teacher must say, "We want *you* but we cannot
have that behavior. You must decide to change it. Make your
decision as quickly as you can, for we want you back again."
Occasionally, depending on the maturity of the students, the class
must discuss what they can do to help a child who does not
know how to control his impulses. This is more effective if the
offender is present.

Some persons are blocked in their emotional development and so remain at an infantile level of behavior. At the age of two or three it is normal for a child to destroy things. Ordinarily, as they grow up they stop taking things apart and prefer to put them together. An immature child may continue to be destructive. Every effort must be made to reward such a child for his more mature behavior until he comes to understand that it is better to act his age than to be a baby.

Constant failure, suppression, repression, rejection at school or at home create hostility. A child who always finds himself in an inferior position, who is ignored and neglected, who feels that no one really cares whether he learns may reach the point where he can no longer contain his anger at such treatment. Then he is likely to strike out at anyone especially if he cannot strike the adults who are the cause of his frustration and distress. In time such a child may develop an overall pattern of violent aggression—striking, attacking, destroying whenever his emotions cannot be otherwise controlled. The classroom teacher must always ask, "How did he get that way? What has been done to him? What is my part in the picture? What have I done too much of, too little of? What must I stop doing? What must I do more? Where do I begin tomorrow morning?"

Not all children react to rejection and failure in the same way. Some withdraw, become silent, apathetic, nonparticipant. For this child, too, the teacher must first find out how he got that way. Other children react to failure and rejection by getting physically sick. Doctors say that probably half the people who come to their offices are suffering from emotionally caused illnesses. The causes of chronic migraines, upset stomachs, spastic colons, allergies, and ulcers may lie in the classroom.

Some successful and controlled children, especially in adolescence, may act in response to a group will. The peer group exerts strong influence on its members. To be in a powerful group, and especially to be its leader, is recognition and acceptance deeply desired by many adolescents. Once an individual achieves such a position he may be pushed into behavior he knows is wrong, but he must consolidate his leadership or lose status. Under such circumstances a "good kid" may act like a sick one. Young people who talk about their use of drugs seem to be saying that the pressure of the group is often too strong to resist.

Teachers who believe that a whipping is the only punishment to which "they" will respond use it more frequently and with less discrimination than many people realize. They say, "Unless we use the paddle those kids will take advantage of us because they think a teacher who doesn't use it is weak and afraid of them. Then they get out of control." Most of the children paddled in school are male and nonwhite. Moreover, school personnel readily admit that most of the children who are whipped once will be whipped again and again. Too many teachers and principals seem not to understand that punitive treatment creates punitive people.

The reasons given for using corporal punishment are varied and often questionable. A young woman, cheeks flaming and eyes blazing, burst into the teachers' lounge. It was dismissal time in a crowded, newly desegregated middle school. The corridor was crowded with young adolescents on their noisy way out. "I just paddled two of 'em," she cried out. "You did? You mean you whipped them?" asked a visiting consultant. "Yes, I did and I'll bet they'll never do that again!" The teacher spoke with heat and conviction. The consultant persisted, "You paddled them? In the corridor?" "No, I took them into a room." "But what for? Why did you hit them? Were they your pupils? Do you know them?" The consultant probed deeper into the situation. The teacher replied, "No, I don't know them! They're not mine! But they were making finger signals and I'll have none of that around here!"

In most elementary schools the principal is usually the one who administers corporal punishment. He is often pressured to do so by the teachers who accuse him of "not backing them up" when he refuses. As a result, principals are anxious to justify their actions and tell of instances in which the results seemed to be good. "Most of the time James could not be controlled in the classroom," said Mr. Williams. "He came to us from another school and the records showed that he had been under treatment for his behavior problems. In fact he was psychotic. His teacher sent him to me over and over and I tried to talk to him but it did no good. He has no parents and has been handed around from one foster home to another, and I knew it was no use to call the present foster mother in. So, at my wits end, I asked the boy if he wanted me to whip him and he said yes. And, you know, after that he was my friend. Every time he saw me he put his arms around me and wanted me to pet him."

The principal was baffled by the experience. He was unable to answer the questions raised by members of the group to whom he had told the story: Should a mentally sick child be whipped? Didn't "beating devils out of the insane" go out of style long years ago? Did the child possibly think that fathers could whip children and still love them? Was the child in search of a father and so asked the principal to play what he thought was the father role? Did he react thereafter as he might have done to a father he believed loved him? Could a father-son relationship have been created in some other way? How would the new relationship with the principal affect the child's behavior in the classroom?

Self-respect is of the greatest importance to every human being. It comes to the child as a result of being treated with respect. If a child has not experienced such an attitude and action in others, especially those who are of significance to him, he comes to believe that he is unworthy of respect, so there is no use even trying to act in a different way. Always the person behaves as he sees himself to be.

In his discussion of the article "Pills for Classroom Peace?" written by Dr. Edward T. Ladd, which appeared in Saturday Review, November 21, 1970, Dr. R. A. Wortman said, ". . . most learning difficulties are reasonably complex, take time and effort to unravel, and much more time to treat.

"For example, taking hyperactivity as the presenting symptom, I have seen among hyperactive children individuals whose condition was (a) post-encephalitic; (b) pre-psychotic; (c) a manifestation of an active defense against depression; (d) an anxious, driven attempt to overcome the limits of modest mental ability in an intellectual school; (e) a manifestation of an 'empty' personality caused by terrible deprivation as a baby; (f) the result of living with an out-of-control alcoholic; (g) the result of living in a genuinely dangerous neighborhood; (h) the result of living with a paranoid father who beat the child; (i) the result of guilty attempts to get punished in school for 'crimes' committed at home; (j) the result of sleeping with a hysterical mother; (k) the result of a neurological deficit with mild family stress (a vulnerable child who probably would have done all right without the stress, as one suspects many do who receive supportive parenting and education); and many more."[1]

Teachers need much more information than they ordinarily have about their out-of-control pupils and much more insight into the causes of behavior. It seems abundantly clear, however, that whipping will not be an effective deterrent or corrective measure for any of the children described by Dr. Wortman.

There is yet another question to be answered. If a child or a teen-ager knows that he will get a whipping as the result of certain actions or, when given a choice, says he wants a whipping, the adult must find out why. All behavior is caused. Among the causes for choosing to be whipped are overall feelings of guilt from which the child or teen-ager must have relief but which may not arise from anything connected with the classroom. Another cause may be masochistic urges of which neither the youngster nor his teacher are aware. The whipping itself will have little effect on either cause, and will, therefore, not be a deterrent to repetition of the offensive behavior.

What the teacher does and says to and about a child provide the child and his classmates with clues from which a picture of self begins to emerge. The individual and his peers begin to question whether he is good, as good as, worth something, worth as much as, worthy of trust, able to learn, a somebody or a nobody. Sometimes teachers seem to be unaware of the effect of their words and actions on a child's thoughts about himself.

A small group of six-year-olds were seated with the teacher at a little table. The teacher was anxious for the observer to see how well the children were learning to read from the Sullivan materials. One child, bored with the slow pace of the work, began to read ahead of the group. The teacher, smiling sweetly at him, said, "I see, Johnny, you are able to work faster than the rest of us." The observer, noticing that the little girl sitting next to her had also moved to the next and the next pages, called that to the teacher's attention. First the teacher frowned and shook her head then she said in a sarcastic, patronizing, babying

---

[1] Letters to the Education Editor, "Drugs and the Disruptive Child," *Saturday Review*, December 19, 1970.

voice, "Oh, is somebody looking on somebody else's book?" One child is praised, the other is shamed. Why? Not only the little girl herself but her classmates must wonder why.

It is obvious that satisfaction of the need to accomplish, to achieve, is critical in the classroom. Every child wants desperately to be successful, to get things right and, when he does so, to be praised and rewarded. This book deals with how to give every child experiences of success despite the fact that they differ so much in levels of development, in skills, in native endowments, in health, in backgrounds. When failure to do what the teacher expects at the same time and in the same quantity as others is added to experiences of rejection, anxiety, and feelings of inferiority and inadequacy, discouragement usually results in apathy, withdrawal, frustration and aggression, or psychosomatic illness. Success and acceptance are essential for they free the energy needed for effort and they motivate learning.

When the consultant entered a first-grade classroom, the young teacher was scolding a child: "There you are again, nothing but scribbling! We can't waste our supplies like that! I'll save this paper for you so that when you want to scribble again you can have it back. I don't see why you can't do what the other children do. Now go sit down and get to work!" The little boy went to his desk, put his head on his arms, and did not get to work.

The consultant questioned the teacher about the child and his behavior. "He is often absent," she said, "and when he does come, he often runs home in the middle of the morning. His father deserted several years ago. His mother is an alcoholic." With a little help and thought the teacher began to see that the child's absence could be caused by the mother's failure to get up in the morning and that when he ran home it might be to reassure himself that no one had taken her away. The teacher also began to see that the child must surely be in a highly anxious state and possibly angry because she did not help him bear his very great burden of fear.

Presently the consultant saw the child reach under his desk for a piece of paper and a crayon. She said to the teacher, "Look, he is going to do something (possibly scribble?). Why don't you go to him? Put your arm around him, give him a hug and say, I'm so glad you decided to work. I've come over to help you." Later in the day the teacher, her face glowing with pleasure,

showed the consultant the child's paper. He had printed a
story about his cat and before leaving had said, "It isn't finished.
"I'll come back and make a picture for it." The teacher had
conveyed by her tone of voice, by her words, and through contact that she cared about the child and would go out of her way
to give him personal help.

In addition to experiencing all that characterizes warm, accepting, understanding human relationships, children at all age
levels must have many opportunities to learn about the underlying emotions and values that cause people to behave well or
badly toward each other. The study of basic human needs must
become part of literature, language arts, social studies, courses
in social issues and problems of democracy and, of course, the
humanities.

Goodwin Watson in his book *What Psychology Can We Trust*,
N.Y.: Teachers College Press 1961, said:

"An autocratic atmosphere, produced by a dominating
teacher who controls direction via intricate punishments,
produces in learners apathetic conformity, various and frequently devious kinds of defiance—scapegoating (venting
hostility, generated by the repressive atmosphere, on col-
leagues), or escape (psychologically or physically) . . . produces
increasing dependence on authority, with consequent obsequi-
ousness, anxiety, shyness and acquiescence.

. . . conventional schools and classrooms condemn most
learners to continuing criticism, sarcasm, discouragement and
failure so that self confidence, aspiration . . . and a healthy self
concept are destroyed. Whitehead called the process 'soul
murder'.

"Learners condemned to relentless failure learn only that
they cannot learn and their anger and distress . . . are frequently vented against the society that has inflicted this
inhuman punishment on them."

3 LEARNING

"In too many classrooms today (there is) little joy, fun and excitement in learning, domination by routines, not spirit. We need to spread the range of experiences, to teach children *how to learn* as well as *what to learn* and foster in them the excitement in discovery of new learnings."

Alice Keliher
"Talks With Teachers"
Darien, Conn., The Educational Publishing Corp. 1958

Learning to Learn

As soon as he comes into the world every human being begins to learn about himself, other people, and the world in which he lives through the use of his five senses—eyes, ears, nose, mouth and touch. The learning begins and continues with or without formal teaching by the parents. If there is encouragement and help, the child learns more, faster and more easily, and his curiosity grows. If his parents and others call his attention to what is around him and attach words to his experiences, he develops a fairly large vocabulary in a surprisingly short time.

Constant feedback from those around the child helps him to learn how best to use the words he knows so as to convey his thoughts and needs to them. The grammatical constructions he begins to use are those he hears in his home and neighborhood. This is now designated the "primary language." In the slums and ghettos of the lowest social class, especially if the people are nonwhite, the primary language is highly idiomatic and colloquial. In middle-class families and neighborhoods, it is likely to be more or less standard English.

If parents and others in the child's family provide him with increasing numbers of experiences, interpret their meaning to him, answer his questions, listen while he recalls what has happened or tells about his fantasies, require him to listen when

13

they talk to him, his attention, memory, and imagination develop and his aural and visual perceptions are sharpened. Such skills and abilities are important to the child when he enters school.

Many children come to school at age six handicapped because of lack of language rather than by lack of mental ability. They come from impoverished homes and neighborhoods. Their parents have had little education and neither time nor inclination to spend at home talking to the little ones. Such children may not understand even half the words the teacher uses, and so they cannot learn from her presentations, follow her directions, or obey her orders. Sometimes they cannot connect name words with the objects they represent. Qualifying words are few in the vocabularies of such children, so they cannot describe what they see or their sensations of sound, touch, taste, or smell. This lack of language gets in the way when the teacher wants such a pupil to tell what he thinks or feels or hopes or intends to do or recall what he learned the day before. It retards development of reading, writing, and spelling skills. Teachers all over the nation ask, "What can an ordinary teacher do in an ordinary classroom with no more than traditional materials and equipment to make up for environmental handicaps in language and, at the same time, provide learning experiences for others in the room who differ widely in native abilities as well as developmental levels.

Teachers can do two things that will help: (1) provide direct sensory experiences and (2) teach children how to learn words.

Simple materials assembled in boxes should be available for a child to work with by himself for short periods during the day whenever the ordinary busy work assigned to the class is unproductive or boring. For example, an ordinary shoe box can be filled with things of various textures such as pieces of metal, wood, fur, silk, velvet, paper, carpet. As the child touches, weighs, and feels them, he needs words to describe his sensations: smooth, rough, sharp, cool, silky, grainy. After a while he needs similes to express comparisons: light as a feather, heavy as lead, soft as skin. These words and phrases can be supplied by the teacher, if she is not otherwise engaged, or by the aide, if there is one, or by a more experienced classmate. The words can be printed or written on cards or paper pasted on the articles. The child must be required to repeat the descriptive word whenever he feels the sensation or indicates the thing. He also needs his own card on which the word is printed so he can learn to spell it and read it and file it in his own word box.

Other boxes should be assembled to provide direct sensory experiences. For example, one can be filled with things that make sounds: spoons to clap, rods to tap, a small mouth organ, a reed or metal pipe, a whistle, a little horn, things to rub together. Work with this box as well as times to listen to the sounds outside the window or in the room or building will not only add such words as swish, rumble, smash, crash, bump, screech but will also increase audio perceptions, ability to discriminate and distinguish differences, and skill in using the voice and tongue to make clear sounds.

Similar boxes of materials can be gathered for experiences in tasting, smelling, and looking.

If direct sensory experiences are to be accompanied by learning to read, write and spell, the teacher must teach children *how* to learn words. Sylvia Ashton Warner in her book "The Teacher" published by Simon & Schuster, New York, gives the clue in the method she used to teach Maori children English. Every day, as her pupils came in, each one told her what word he wanted for the day. She printed it on a card and gave it to him. If, as the teacher does this, whether it be the word the child wants for the day or a word he has just gotten from his experience with one of the boxes described above, she says, "Here's your very own word. Will you learn it?" she can get a commitment from the child to do something about learning. When the child answers, "Yes, I will," her next question is "How will you learn it?"

When the teacher has taught children how to learn words, the child can give the following answer:

I will look at it and say it, look at it and say it, over and over.

I will show it to my friends and tell them what it is.

I will take it home, show it to my mother, tell her what it is, and teach it to my sister.

I will spell it and say it.

I will use it in a sentence.

I will trace it with my fingers.

I will write it in the air.

I will close my eyes and see it.

Thus learning is reinforced through several senses. The child sees the word, says it and hears it, touches it, has a kinesthetic experience with it, uses his voice, his memory, and his imagination.

In some cases children can hunt through the stack of magazines the teacher has on a table or in a corner to find an appropriate picture to paste on his word card. The word card should be brought back each day to be filed in each child's personal vocabulary (or language acquisition) box. If an occasional child says, "The dog ate it" or "The baby tore it up," no fuss should be made about it. A new card should be printed for the child to place in his box as soon as he has learned the word.

Whenever a child learns a new word he should record that happy event in the journal or log or diary in which he writes what he learns each day. Word boxes and learning logs are visible evidence of the growth and accomplishments that parents, teachers, and the children want.

Sometimes children do not take part in what the teacher is asking the class to do because the teacher has not asked them to do so. In a first-grade classroom all but two children were gathered near the front board at which the teacher was drawing symbols (circles) to show what happens when addition and subtraction take place. She called upon individuals to go to the board to show that they had learned what it was all about. Two children, a boy and a girl, both black, were not with the group. They had left their places without remonstrance by the teacher. The little girl was playing at a small chalk board at the rear of the room. The boy was seated not too far away watching her. The consultant asked the girl why she had left the group. She said, "Cos she never lets me do it." "Do what?" the consultant prodded. "At the board," was her answer. Then the consultant went to the boy who had not heard the previous conversation with the girl. "Why did you come away from the teacher and the other children?" the consultant asked. He answered, "I never get to go." "Go where? What do you mean?" she asked. The boy, like the girl, said, "Go to the board like the others do." Presently, one by one, four or five other children detached themselves from the group going back to join the black children. An animated little circle was soon engaged in laughing and talking together. The teacher kept right on teaching, ignoring the withdrawal and the sound of voices from the rear of the room.

In many secondary school classrooms observers will see boys and sometimes girls with their heads down on their desks. They may be sleeping or merely so bored or frustrated they can no longer endure watching the teacher and listening to his voice. Teachers ignore this behavior most of the time, make no attempts to involve the boys, and say they have no time to find out the reasons for their withdrawal. Yet it is important to know. Is such a boy really tired because he got up at three A.M. to deliver newspapers or because he worked until midnight at the gas station? Does he lack proper rest because he shares his bed with three siblings in a noisy, crowded home? Is he sick? Or possibly using drugs? Do such students withdraw because they are bored by having to listen to the teacher repeat in dull fashion what they already know or because they do not understand half the words the teacher uses and are too frustrated to continue to listen? Teachers who are uninformed or indifferent to causes or hostile to minority group and lower class children usually conclude that such pupils have "low IQ's," lack potential for success in school, and are bound to "fail in life."

Among the children thus far described are some who take no part whatever in what goes on in the classroom. Some of them as well as some who are not handicapped by poverty simply sit by—passive and idle, their eyes vacant or full of dreams. Some find things to play with or to eat. They may hum softly to themselves or constantly talk aloud to themselves or to no one in particular. Occasionally one gets up to wander around the room, to crawl on the floor, or to leave for an aimless walk in the corridor. These pupils are, in fact, quite divorced from the learning process. They do not know that *they* have any responsibility for learning, that *they* must *do* something in order to learn. Unless they can become involved in learning, they are likely to remain detached throughout their years in school. They are the people who, together with their parents, blame the teacher for their failure to learn to read. They say, "You are bad teachers. You have not *taught* us how to read." What they should say is "You have not taught us *how to learn*."

4 LEARNING CENTERS

A child is not fettered by the infinite. For even beyond forever lies discovery . . . that begins when a mind asks, "Why?" This "why", repeated time and again, has led man down incredible avenues of adventure. And knowledge begets knowledge, with each new discovery dovetailing and complementing the last.

Lockheed Aircraft Corporation
Vista, May/June, 1970

Learning Centers

Each learning center described in the following pages includes far more equipment for many more activities than most teachers can manage at one time and more than children could profitably use. Only a few pupils, maybe only two or four, can work at one center at any one time, so a relatively small number of items are required. Once all who need to work there have had a chance, the items must be changed. Each center can be as simple or as complex as the teacher and pupils are able to handle.

The time and work involved in creating and caring for the centers should be shared by the several teachers planning to use them. Schedules for their use can be set weekly according to the teachers' diagnoses of pupil needs. A more complete description of the teacher's role will follow.

Availability and effective use of teacher aides or para-professionals will increase the successful use of direct learning centers. If they are not available, parent volunteers should be sought. Many adults in every community are willing and eager to share their free time with teachers in order to help children learn. The teacher's guiding principle may well be "Never do anything yourself that an aide or a child can do." The results may not be as perfect as those the teacher could produce, but perfection is not the objective; learning is.

When teachers are asked, "How do children learn?," they are likely to ponder a while and then say, "Do you mean how do they study?" The fact is that after grade three "studying" that may not result in learning becomes the way of life for school children. They are told that they will learn if they listen to what the teacher tells them to do; copy the lesson from the board or book; memorize what is on the printed page; find the answers to the questions at the end of the chapter by rereading it; write the answers in the notebook; memorize them; say them when they get a question in class; and check them or write them on test papers. Thus, for most children learning is something that has to do with lessons and exercises, with doing homework, with reading the textbook, with repetition and drill, with listening to the teacher, with repeating his words or giving back to him what the book says. It is something you do to get a mark. It isn't supposed to be any fun.

Learning activities so described can be productive of academic progress for some pupils but for many are sadly unproductive—

To learn by listening.

especially for pupils handicapped in their early childhood by their lack of preparation for school.

Teachers often say, "I am an ordinary teacher in a traditional building, in a classroom that resembles a box; what can I do to break through the usual unproductive classroom routines and procedures? How can I change the children's day from one spent in listening to me talk (I know I often not only ask all the questions but answer them too); in looking at a printed page (which I know too many of them can't read); in copying letters or words from workbooks or board (whether or not they convey any meaning); in coloring in outline forms and figures using hard stubs of crayons which cramp the fingers and increase tensions (an exercise that has neither artistic nor educational value); in sitting on the sidelines, feeling ignored and left out; in experiencing the devastating effects of inadequacy, incompetence, and failure?"

The following suggestions for learning activities are offered in the hope that by using them teachers will be able to shift emphasis from teaching to learning. They are not intended as a substitute for reading or arithmetic, for content courses or useful drills. Their use is intended to supplement subject matter not to replace it. They will help the teacher to provide individualized learning experiences which children need and from which, according to his need, each will learn more about himself, about his world, and especially about how to learn.

The proposal is to create learning centers where pupils will have direct sensory experiences to which words and ideas can be attached, where concepts can be formed, curiosity increased, and the skills of learning to learn developed. Nine possible types of learning centers are described, but the teacher needs not be limited to them. It is unlikely that the ordinary classroom will provide enough space for all of them at the same time. How many can be accommodated will depend on the size of the room, the number of pupils, the kind of furniture, the ingenuity of the teacher, and his skill in organization and management. As soon as pupils develop enough leadership, enough individual and group controls, and the dependability needed to work without constant teacher supervision, centers can be placed in adjacent corridors, preparation rooms, resource centers, materials rooms, seldom used offices, and corners of the library.

How to Use Learning Centers

THE TEACHER'S ROLE

Children have to be taught what the learning centers are for and how to use them. This is the teacher's first responsibility and may have to be. repeated many times, sometimes for the whole class, other times for individuals or groups. It will help if, as they are developed, guidelines are printed on a large chart to be kept visible for those who need reminders. (One way to do the essential language learning for which the centers provide direct sensory experiences is the routine for learning new words fully described on pages 15–16.)

To recapitulate: a supply of cards should always be at hand. When a child uses a word to name an article or describe a sensation, the teacher or teacher-aide or a pupil at the center prints or writes it (or does both) on a card, which he gives to the child as his very own word for the day. As the pupil takes the word-card, he must answer in the affirmative the question, "Will you learn it?" And he must tell how he will do so.

Another objective for which learning centers are designed is to develop curiosity, imagination, and memory. Therefore, the teacher or aide must always ask specific questions as a child examines and uses whatever he finds of interest at the center. These also can be printed on a guide chart and kept at eye level for pupils to see. The heading can be "Questions I Need to Answer." The children should raise the questions; they are likely to be:

What is it called?

Have I ever seen it before? Where?

How does it taste or feel or smell?

What does it remind me of?

Can I find something like it at home, or outside, or in the box?

Is it beautiful?

What could I do with it?

What have I learned about it to put in my learning book?

PLANS

What plans are made will depend very much on the maturity and experience levels of the pupils. However, daily planning is essential for the orderly and successful use of learning centers. One item to go into the plan is the time schedule, and it should indicate a specific time for writing in the log and sharing learnings with classmates. Everything a child records and shares should be received with pleasure and praise by the teacher and the group. The variation in length, that is, quantity of learning, done by different children should not be discussed with the class. No matter how much or how little a child learns, the teacher must praise and reward it. A handshake is one way to congratulate a pupil on his success. Another way is for the class to give one clap. Everyone should understand that learning is not a competition and that one child is not to be compared with another. Teacher and pupils must know that a child who learns as much as he can is not a failure even though what he learns may be less than what a classmate learned. *Every child is a winner when he learns.*

Learning logs, which individuals may want to call diaries or books or records, will help both teachers and parents become aware of a child's rate and style of learning. They are also invaluable diagnostic tools. Children should be encouraged to take them home to share with their families if there is a reasonable chance of their safe return.

In addition to records of learnings parts of these books can be used for other purposes. For example, in one section children may write "Questions I want to get answered" or "Things I want to find out" or "What I discovered today" or "Today I saw (or did) for the first time" or "Today I had a new idea."

PUPIL PARTICIPATION IN DECISION MAKING

Planning is another skill essential to effective living in our society. The planning process requires an individual to be skilled in making decisions. Most children get a chance to practice making decisions only outside of the classroom for they are not given choices or options or alternatives from which to choose the learning experiences of most importance to them. The use of learning centers in the ordinary classroom presents many opportunities for children to make important decisions.

For example, when the teacher first tells the class about the direct sensory experiences that he intends to make available to them, ample time should be allowed for the children to raise questions about how and when they can be used and to talk about what should be placed in each one. As they offer suggestions, the teacher should write them on the chalk board and be careful to accept all even though a few may be bizarre or unreasonable. At a later time the children should review their first ideas and eliminate whatever is unobtainable or irrelevant. If this procedure is followed, no child will feel rejected when he participates because what he has offered does not suit the teacher. After a lapse of time no one will remember who suggested the items classmates now want to drop out.

Another time for pupils to enter the process of decision making is when it comes time to replace centers that have been sufficiently used. (This presupposes that the space available is not sufficient to accommodate more than two or three.) The teacher, of course, also participates in preliminary discussions; for he must make sure that everyone gets equal opportunity to express his ideas and also that everything relevant has been explored. However, at no time in any planning activity should the teacher resort to manipulation or subterfuge or pretense in order to influence the outcome. If he does, the pupils will lose faith in his sincerity and take little part thereafter.

Every day the pupils can decide what part of the day they want reserved to use the learning centers. Flexibility of scheduling is preferable to setting a rigid time slot for their use. Weather conditions, which affect children's moods, school-wide programs and activities, and other learning experiences that the teacher must include in the daily program, should be taken into consideration by the children when they are making decisions. Responsibility for deciding how much of the day should be devoted to the centers (as a total class activity) remains with the teacher who has to consider other instructional needs.

When it is time to use the centers, each child should decide for himself what he is to do. The options or alternatives must be clearly understood. For example, there is the possibility of a child remaining at his own desk to do a task in which he is interested. If sensory boxes are also available, some pupils may prefer working with them individually or in pairs. Someone may want to begin or to go on with an independent learning project in the library or (if the school provides them) in a resource center elsewhere in the building. The corridor is another place for one or several pupils to work together. The teacher has not only the right but the responsibility to make suggestions to individuals in the light of what he knows to be their learning needs. He must also have at hand records of where individuals have worked on previous days in order to prevent aggressive pupils from monopolizing any one center at the expense of more timid classmates.

As center groups form, the pupils in each group should decide which one of them is to be leader-for-the-day. That child must be able and willing to accept responsibility for helping to control the noise level, for helping to resolve interpersonal disputes over the use of materials, and for securing cooperation from the others in putting things in order before leaving the center. Academic abilities are not needed for the jobs of the center leader and need not be taken into account when making a choice. Thus, slow learners and retarded readers will also have a chance to be selected by their peers for this prestige position which involves practice of leadership skills.

TRAINING LEADERS

As soon as possible, group leaders should be chosen by the members of the group. In the beginning, however, it would be well for the teacher to prepare some of the most able and reliable pupils for that responsibility. The necessary instruction can be given to these children in a group when the others are at work on other assignments. Their duties should include checking each center to be sure there are word cards ready for use, that a sharpened pencil is available, and that worn-out materials are removed. They can be expected to call the teacher's attention to a center that needs to be replenished.

MATERIALS

Limitations of space and problems of control usually make it necessary to permit only a few children to be at any one center at a time. This helps to keep the number of needed items to a reasonable amount. As soon as all the pupils have used them, a new and different supply can be placed there. Pupil leaders, teacher aides, and the teacher may have to make records of materials and of who used them. It is essential that pupils be in contact with more and more things, learn more and more words, and develop their powers of observation more and more fully.

OTHER OPPORTUNITIES

Since all pupils cannot use the learning centers at the same time, the teacher must plan for other learning activities. If learning boxes are available, individuals or pairs can work with them either at their own desks or in a corner of the room on the floor. Children are comfortable on the floor. Small mats or pieces of carpet will help. The most able children, especially those who have not lacked the early sensory experiences which the centers and boxes are designed to supply and who are not busy with leadership responsibilities, should be permitted to use this time for independent learning projects which may take them to the library or to a resource center or to a single desk or small table placed in the corridor. In some innovative schools, this is called an "open classroom."

When individuals and small groups are at work doing many different things according to their needs and interests, one-to-one relationships are easily set up. The teacher, the aide, the able pupil designated as an assistant to the teacher can sit down beside a child who needs help to teach reading, spelling, or numbers; to work with him in manipulating concrete materials needed to establish number concepts; to play word games, to drill with word, sentence, or number flash cards.

Small committees organized for special purposes can gather around tables or in circles and meet at this time. They may want to plan, pool their findings, report to each other, get help from the teacher, or prepare progress and final reports to be given to the class. If small groups are working on a dramatization, this is the time when they can rehearse—in the corridor if it is necessary to reduce the number of pupils in the room.

Individual pupils may use this time for assigned housekeeping chores. These include book circulation and return, organizing and filing clippings and other resource materials, renewing bulletin board displays, keeping storage closets in order, checking on needed supplies. These tasks and chores should be shared by all the pupils on a rotating basis. It is essential that they not be done solely by the slower learners or minority group children.

TIME KEEPING

Although the pupils should participate in making decisions about the use of the centers, the teacher is responsible for determining how much time is to be given to them each day. He is guided by his awareness of other learning activities the class must have. He keeps track of time and announces when it is time to stop work at the centers (and elsewhere in the room); reminds the pupils of their responsibility for putting things in order before leaving; and asks them to return quickly to their desks or tables.

Just before the learning centers are to be used each day, it may, for some weeks, be necessary for the teacher to remind the children of what they are to do and again and again to emphasize the necessity of learning to learn with eyes, ears, nose, mouth, and touch. Some pupils will need more repetition than others. Some may be able to tell the others that their jobs are to learn to say, spell, read, and write words, and to discover new facts they did not know before. The teacher will need to reassure children that they can talk to each other about their discoveries and their ideas. Some will need frequent reminder to have something to write in their learning logs at the end of the day. It will help all to know what the noise signal is and that it means lower voices are desired.

Classrooms in which children are free to go to various parts of the room to find and use materials from which to learn what they feel a need for and/or a desire to learn, are often called *open classrooms*. The following outline may help the reader to visualize what the room looks like.

Furniture includes:
  —open book cases used to divide rooms into learning areas.
  —chairs—straight, tablet arms, individual desk units, rockers, stools.
  —floor covering—carpet, scatter "rugs" (pieces of carpet).
  —tables—large work, 4 × 6, round.
  —individual units and/or small table, chairs in corridors.

Areas of learning include as many of following as possible:
  —reading area—wall of open book shelves. Two sides of open square made up of book cases, rug on floor, small table, rocking chair, and straight chair.
  —arithmetic area—small table, box of counters, flash cards, abacus, cuisinaire rods, number games.
  —game area—carpet on floor, boxes of games, checkers, jigsaw puzzles, word cards.
  —magazine corner—stack of magazines, scissors, paste, file box, carpet.
  —sensory experience area—tables or shelves on which are boxes of materials for learning through eyes, ears, nose, touch, taste.
  —listening area—table and chair, record player and records, tape recorder, casettes, ear phones, T.V., radio.
  —seeing area—film strip projector, pictures, post card collections, slides, reading machines, T.V.

In addition to opening the classroom the entire school is being opened by making it possible for pupils to go outside to learn by:

  —*taking walks*—in nearby gardens, woods, fields to observe plant and animal life, soil, water and to gather specimens to bring back for study.
  —*talking to people*—elder citizens about the past family life, folk lore, struggles, difficulties connected with retirement.
  —*visiting museums*—to study artifacts, letters, photographs, clothing, art treasures, historical documents.
  —*going to headquarters*—of various lands or organizations (social, labor, political, fraternal, welfare, information) to

learn about reasons for their existence, purposes, histories, membership, methods.

—*and to businesses and industries*—service, distribution, communication, transportation to see operations, find out about kinds of jobs, qualifications, pay scales, reason for firing, ways to secure promotion.

—*inviting resource persons*—to come in from all walks of life to talk to large and small groups on specific subjects and to be questioned by students in terms of their interests and needs.

—*listening to speakers*—assemblies and classroom groups representing all ethnic and racial groups, all professions and occupations, government officials, and political leaders.

—*using resource centers, activity rooms, and laboratories*— to which individuals or small groups can go in otherwise unassigned time or instead of classes in which study, drill exercises, teacher lectures, or discussions are scheduled which they do not need. These may be the library or rooms equipped for clay modeling, painting, cooking, sewing, crafts, wood work, metal, electrical work, science, social studies, writing.

OBSERVATION

Whenever learning centers are in use, the teacher must take time to visit in order to observe pupils as they work. He needs to watch what a child does with things; to listen to what he says about them; to encourage him to tell how he feels about the experiences he is having; to answer his questions; to direct his attention to what he has not yet noticed; to recognize and praise his success. These visits are opportunities for the teacher to make diagnostic and evaluative notes about individual pupils. His records of growth and progress, rates and styles of learning, and instructional needs still to be met will be important when parents want reports or come for conferences.

5 LEARNING TO LEARN

"Instruction is . . . the process of guiding and directing the experiences of children to the end that they learn. . . . Classrooms . . . should cease to be lesson-hearing rooms. Rather they should be centers where children engage in the activities that will lead to the learning that is socially desirable."

Anderson, Whipple and Gilchrist
"The School As A Learning Laboratory"
The National Society for the Study of Education
49th Year Book, Part 1

More About Learning to Learn Centers

I—LEARNING TO LEARN BY USING ALL THE SENSES

At this center the teacher and the children accumulate all kinds of material things that the pupils can touch, smell, taste, look at, listen to. Some like to call the big carton or can used to hold them a "magnificent junk box." It can be a permanent fixture in one corner of any classroom. The children will enjoy decorating it, and, because they enjoy using it as a place to learn new words from new experience, they are not likely to desecrate it. Responsibility for keeping it well filled, for removing used up or worn out articles, and for keeping it orderly should be allocated on a rotating basis to the pupils.

The "junk" should consist of pieces of wood, metal, paper, fur, and textiles from which to learn about textures, relative weights, grain, and color. Small containers filled with samples of soils, rocks, stones, leaves, grasses, tree bark, flowers, nuts, seeds, and insects should be there to open up the things nature provides for people to enjoy. Items that can be borrowed from home or the custodian or the science laboratory include tools, bells, wires, small musical instruments, locks, and keys. Spices, seasoning, herbs, perfumes, soap, powders will provide new smelling and tasting experiences. Eyes, ears, nose, mouth, and fingers will be used more and more effectively as the skills of examining, observing, hearing are developed and what the psychologist calls audio and visual perceptions become sharper.

Direct sensory experiences will give children new awareness of self and increasing joy in living as well as confirmation of their ability to learn. Much attention needs to be given to the words with which the experiences can be described. Depending upon the maturity of the pupils, each new word a child learns to say can be printed or written for or by him on a card which he can put into his own "word box." These are the words each one learns to read by looking at them many times, by spelling them, by showing them to friends and parents, by tracing over the letters, by pretending to write them in the air, and by using them. As more and more words are added to the vocabulary, pride in personal accomplishment and feelings of success replace apathy and indifference to learning. Comparison of one child to another should be avoided by the teacher. The important element is learning, not quantity. If there are children in the class who speak Spanish or Navaho or Hopi or any other language, learning words at the "junk box" may give them opportunities to teach their words to their English-speaking classmates.

When the pupils are ready for it, articles can be sorted, classified and categorized; this will add new dimensions to their learning. Children can also be encouraged to create by combining things and inventing ways to use them. Later in the day, when it is time for conversation, the experiences at the learning center can be described. Thus memory is trained.

II—LEARNING ABOUT THE SELF (ME)

This center is designed to provide experiences which will help to create positive feelings about the self—a positive concept or self-image. It is especially important for disadvantaged non-white pupils who often have feelings of inferiority, inadequacy, incompetence, and inability to learn. A negative self-image inhibits learning and must be dispelled. Some of the elements in the black child's concept of self grow out of the racial experience which, in this country, has been exclusion, rejection, restriction, and segregation. Some of it comes from parents who do not know how to inspire the child with self-confidence or who transmit their own despair of attaining success. Some of it grows out of the widespread attitude that fair skin and blue eyes are most beautiful and advantageous. And some of it is embedded in the values attached to color words—white is right, pure, better than; black is dangerous, evil, of lesser value. The recent adoption of the slogan, black is beautiful, is wholesome and should be accepted and promoted by the school teacher who at the same time must teach that beauty is more than skin deep.

The first requisite for this center then is a good large mirror; for some children of poverty may never have seen true pictures of themselves. There may be no mirrors at home, or at best they may be cracked or of such poor quality that they distort the face. In our middle class society cleanliness is considered not only "next to godliness" but also an adjunct to beauty. The center should therefore be located where there is a wash basin. An orange crate makes an excellent dressing table. A shelf or a small cabinet built in the school shop should be erected nearby to hold soap and paper towels. A shoeshine box would be useful. Needle, thread, and buttons would also help with grooming problems. Small individual boxes made in class or brought from home will be needed to hold personal articles like combs, nail files, hair and tooth brushes, ribbons and hair pins, nail polish, hand lotion, and deodorants. A box of materials of many colors should be there for pupils to see how color either adds to or detracts from the beauty of one's skin color. Every effort must be made to help children of all complexions to appreciate their own and each other's skin color. The slogan, black is beautiful, is a good one for both races. This center is the place where both boys and girls can try various ways of arranging the hair and can learn that color and styles of clothing can enhance good points and minimize bad. A tape measure and scales will help pupils to keep track of growth and deal with problems of weight.

This is also the learning center where pupils can try on various facial expressions to see how they affect the beholder. As they see emotions on their own and classmates' faces, they learn something about coping with self and others. Conversation periods can provide opportunity to continue this learning by talking about the causes of fear, anger, frustration, scorn, indifference, love, hate, happiness, sorrow, displeasure, and despair. Understanding will be increased when human relations and motivations are discussed in connection with their study of poems and stories. Through role-playing pupils can act out their feelings and see the effects of alternate ways of behaving. All these activities extend language, develop the ability to communicate both verbally and nonverbally, and increase the skills of memory and recall.

III—LEARNING TO LEARN BY LOOKING AT PICTURES

If "one picture is worth a thousand words," this center will be productive. Here is the place for all kinds of visual materials and equipment designed to train children to learn by using their eyes and interpreting what they see. A file cabinet or a sturdy carton or box made in the school's shop and fitted with cardboard dividers can be used to hold pictures, posters, maps, and charts of all kinds. Many of them can be cut out of magazines, newspapers, and advertising materials. Quantities are obtainable from industries, businesses, tourist agencies, and airlines. Some can come from government and social agencies. Sets of pictures are usually included in school supply catalogues. Picture postcard collections, photograph albums, books, charts and models of birds, flowers, trees, insects, and animals provide many pictures from which children can get information about the natural and the man-made world in which they live. Very often collections of flora and fauna can be borrowed from local colleges.

Most schools are now equipped with machines that enable children to see pictures more effectively—individual snapshot viewers, slide projectors, small filmstrip projectors, which even second graders can operate or which older students assigned as teacher-aides or parent volunteers can handle for them. Magnifying glasses and simple microscopes will increase opportunities for children to learn by seeing.

Many new words can be added to the speaking and reading vocabularies of children who use this center. From these direct sensory experiences pupils will get much to talk about and to recall when they talk to their parents about what they are learning in school.

IV—LEARNING TO LEARN BY LISTENING AND HEARING

This center is especially aimed at increasing perception of sounds which children may have learned to screen out. It is the place for equipment such as tape recorders and tapes, record players and discs, small radios, and TV's. Head sets for individual listening are essential for pupils who need to hear over and over again in order to learn. (See photograph on page 19.) If the teacher tapes as he teaches, any child can hear the lesson as often as necessary. Teachers, parents, librarian, and aides can record the stories and poems they read to the class which some children will enjoy so much that they will want to hear them over and over again. Commercial records of songs children love and of music with which they should become familiar are available in many schools. Use of the center should not be limited to recreation or to enrichment or to time when there is nothing else to do because other work is finished. It must become a primary center for learning especially for pupils who are ear-minded.

If children can tape the stories they want to tell each other and then listen to those recordings, the center will become a place where pupils improve their voices, their diction and pronunciation, and their language usage and learn to communicate more fully by using sentences instead of single words.

The center can be the place where an able reader reads to classmates; where he has opportunities to use his reading skills and share his reading abilities. This is highly motivating. The conditions that must be enforced here will also provide practice in implementing democratic rights—the rights to speak, to be heard, and to hear. Children thus learn to curb impulsive talking and to understand that the individual and the group share responsibility for giving everyone equal opportunity to learn by listening.

Sound makers have a place in this center though their use may depend upon other things happening in the room. As children listen to bells, pipes, mouth organs, flutes, whistles, and drums they can learn to discriminate, describe, name, and enjoy new experiences. Later the new words can be spelled, used and read, and the experiences related to others.

Aural perception, listening skills, and language acquisition are so important in school, especially for the so-called disadvantaged pupils, that more time and attention need to be given them than the center can provide. The following suggestions are offered as guidelines for planning such learning activities as may be required.

1. *Basic concepts.*
   —Listening puts a person in touch with other people and with the phenomenon of sound.
   —communication with and between people depends on learning to listen and to understand what is said.
   —language development depends upon listening.
   —people *hear* different things though they may listen to the same sounds.
   —following directions depends upon listening.
   —the individual learns to screen out sounds he doesn't want to hear. This includes the mother's and the teacher's voices.
   —economically disadvantaged children often have not been required to listen and have not developed a high degree of aural perception.
   —children with hearing defects have difficulty with listening.
   —listening to and producing many and varied sounds will add enjoyment and fun to life.

2. *Abilities and skills which need to be developed.*
   —the ability to hear word endings.
   —the ability to hear parts of words (phonics).
   —the ability to describe sounds.
   —the ability to repeat sounds and words accurately.
   —the ability to follow ever more complicated spoken directions.

3. *Materials needed.*
   —voices, tongues, ears, feet, hands, bells, tuning fork, musical instruments such as reed pipes, tambourines, mouth organ.
   —victrola and records.
   —radio.
   —T.V.
   —sticks, rulers, pencils (for tapping), word flash cards.
   —magazines from which to cut pictures for word cards.
   —paste, scissors.

4. *Kinds of sounds children should learn to hear, distinguish, name, describe, and produce.*
   —different voice sounds: low and high pitch, soft and loud volume, whisper, murmur, pleasant and unpleasant, harsh, smooth, yelling, shouting, calling.

—different noises: banging, dashing, swishing, scratching, smashing, drumming.

—different rythmic sounds: clapping, tapping, stepping, skipping, running, galloping, trotting.

5. *Teaching-learning activities.*

Before planning new learning activities, the teacher must find out what skills and how much language development each child already has.

To do this the teacher and pupils *individually* should make sounds and say the words that name and describe what they hear.

New experiences and the new words needed can then be included in plans for succeeding days.

Experiences through which children learn to listen and hear include the following:

—whispering games. The first child on each row whispers something to the second and so on until the whisper reaches the last child. Then the last child tells what he heard, so does the middle one; anyone who heard something different tells it. Then the child who began tells what he said.

—the windows are opened and the children listen to sounds from outside: the wind, people calling, dogs barking, auto engines running, cars rolling, horns blowing. New words are spoken and learned such as: swish, yelp, shout, murmur, howl, toot, hoot.

—the children tell about sounds they heard on the way to school: auto engines and horns, hammering, people talking, feet walking or running. The new words are written on the board, in the books, and are spelled and used.

—learning to listen to, remember, and follow directions. The teacher (and then individual children as they are ready) tells "a story" which tells someone to do something; at first it may be only one sentence. Children do what they hear. The directions become more complex and require more than one sentence. The stories begin to tell children to do several things. These become more complex. Thus children learn to follow oral directions. Whenever it is appropriate classroom and school rules of behavior in halls, play area, or cafeteria are told to children, are individually repeated, and are practiced.

—everyday for a short time (it is a good way to end the day) the teacher reads a story to the children. Sometimes they act out what they have heard. Stories can be recorded on tape and made available for individual listening.

—from first grade on children enjoy listening to languages other than English and learning to say words, phrases, and sentences used in simple conversation. Foreign language records can be used for this.

—radio and T.V. provide many varied listening experiences. From them children learn to say words, sing jingles, tell stories, act out emotions, and follow directions.

—instead of workbook busy-work children can be paired to practice pronouncing new sounds and sound words. Word cards on which an appropriate picture has been pasted can be used for small group as well as one-to-one practice periods.

V—LEARNING TO LEARN BY TALKING

This center provides a place where it is right to talk. Here the children can enjoy telling each other riddles, jokes, stories, limericks, poems, jingles, their out-of-school experiences, their feelings at home, the happenings in the neighborhood, their hopes and fears, joys and sorrows, and their plans. The older the pupils, the more they want to talk to each other. Conversation skills and the ability to relate to another person need to be developed. This is especially important when the group is mixed racially, religiously, ethnically, or across social-class lines.

Flash cards and tape recordings for letter and letter combination sounds (phonics) should be available at this center so that children can work on their skills individually or in pairs or with the help of an aide. Numerical symbols and number combinations, also on cards, should be there for study and drill.

As children in a socially mixed group talk to each other, it soon becomes evident that their speech and usage patterns differ. Under the guidance of the teacher or an aide they can have fun exchanging their ways of saying the same things. They can learn to recognize some patterns as idiomatic or colloquial (such as "I be there") and others as standard English (such as "I was there").

If Spanish-speaking children, Indians, or any who are bilingual are present, they should be encouraged to teach their words to classmates. This helps to establish equality of status in the mixed peer group as well as pride in one's own primary language. Bilingualism becomes an asset rather than a liability.

VI—LEARNING TO LEARN BY READING

Here the objective is to use reading in order to learn rather than to learn to read. Here the child learns for himself rather than for the teacher. A child should be able to go to this center because he wants to be with books and to read as he pleases without criticism or comment from the teacher. Reading matter attractive to children and of all levels of difficulty should be available so that able readers can have fun reading easy books and also using hard books to get information they may want or need. Slow learners may want to struggle with hard books without threat from anyone, or they may seek help without censure from a classmate or an aide. In addition to books there should be comics, cartoons, magazines, newspapers, pamphlets, dictionaries, and reference books.

There is, of course, another part of the problem of learning by reading and that is learning to read. A child who needs to improve his skill in order to find out what he wants to know should be encouraged to make more and better use of the machines that are now available for that purpose in many schools. These are machines designed to increase eye span, speed, and comprehension. Pupils from grade three or four have little difficulty in learning to operate them.

VII—LEARNING TO LEARN BY DOING

This should be a place where children can use their hands to construct, to take apart, to create. The kinds of things needed include sewing materials, possibly a sewing machine, even a mobile stove, cooking utensils, and food stuffs. There should be pictures for use in making posters and bulletin board displays, and in illustrating word and sentence cards, notebooks, and independent learning projects. Scissors, paste, cardboard, and construction paper will also be needed.

Sometimes this center should be equipped just for art work with paper, paints, pencils, charcoal and crayons, clay, plasticine, soap and wood for carving and whittling, and the tools and materials for block printing, finger painting, paper craft, and leather craft. Some teachers also supply unusual materials for making useful or decorative articles. These include paper cups, tin cans, corks, wooden beads, wooden spoons and spatulas, paper plates of various sizes, spaghetti in various shapes and sizes, crushed egg shells, scrap lumber and plywood, tools, nails, and tacks.

Many toys that children of poverty never get a chance to use are especially designed to provide experiences in taking things apart and putting them together again or in constructing big things out of small ones or from bits and pieces. These, puzzles, and games should also be in this center.

Doing involves so many things that the whole nature of this place can be changed every few weeks. Among the important outcomes to be expected from its use are increases in skill, confidence in one's ability to learn to learn, lengthened attention spans, increasing ability to follow directions, and development of small muscle coordination.

At times the center can be devoted to hobbies, and children can display and explain their own collections of coins, stamps, baseball pictures, rocks, dolls, leaves, insects, buttons, and other objects they love to possess. Curiosity will be stimulated for some, for others the ability to classify, sort, categorize, and organize.

VIII—LEARNING TO LEARN BY WRITING

In this place children should be free to practice writing letters and words, sentences and paragraphs, compose notes to friends or parents, create stories and poems just because they want to. Those who cannot yet write will need letter forms and blocks. Those who want to practice handwriting will need samples to copy.

Letter writing will be encouraged if each child has his own mailbox. These can be made from milk cartons by cutting off the top, wrapping the box in silver paper, and hanging a sign with the owner's name on it. A stack of such boxes resembles the post office. Teacher can put in the mailboxes her welcome back notes for absentees and notes she wants carried home to parents. Children can put in them birthday cards, friendly notes to classmates, and notes to the teacher and to their parents.

What the children write at this center should not be graded, especially if they are open-end questions which the teacher has suggested; neither should these personal matters be read to the class. The teacher, however, will get considerable insight into what makes a child tick from reading papers in which children express their hopes and fears, their doubts and concerns.

The center for writing, of course, must have paper and pencils and pens. Teachers find it helpful to give each pupil a folder in which he can keep his personal writings, his creative work, the writing tasks assigned by the teacher, and his English drills and exercises. These folders should be in a filing box or cabinet accessible to any child when he wants to work in the writing center. As the teacher finds time to do so, he reads the papers in a folder, confers with the individual pupil about them, and provides additional exercises and drill work as needed. These folders are very helpful when the parent arrives to discuss his child's progress. Since all the written work a child does remains in the folder for the entire term, growth is easily seen and measured.

IX—LEARNING TO LEARN BY ROLE-PLAYING OR DRAMATIZING

This center and the activities that go on there help children to learn about self and about human relations. They may engage in spontaneous dramatics reproducing the stories, nursery rhymes, fairy tales, and fables they know and love. They may practice acting parts in the skits they write. They may role-play the psychological and sociological situations they and their classmates experience from day to day. Thus small children try out various roles in order to learn what it feels like to be grown-up. Adolescents, through role reversal, come to a better understanding of what makes their adults tick and of their own behavior. Pretending to be someone else, assuming a different name or accent, behaving in a different way, responding in an unaccustomed fashion are ways in which pupils of all age levels and abilities can learn about human behavior—what motivates people, how words affect actions, how consequences are related to the decisions they make about their own behavior, and how those decisions are affected by the values they hold.

At this center pupils should find puppets which are especially helpful to younger children in acting out their feelings about classmates, school, teacher, and parents.

6 LEARNING TO LEARN IN SECONDARY SCHOOLS

". . . Learning, like all other experiencing and behaving, is an active process which results from the efforts of the individual to satisfy his needs."

Donald Syngg and Arthur Combs
"Individual Behavior"
N.Y. Harper & Brothers, 1949

Study hall.

Learning to Learn in the Secondary School

Many junior and senior high schools across the nation remain untouched by the wave of innovations stimulated by rising demands that teachers account for the illiteracy of their students and graduates. Many secondary school teachers, especially teachers of academic subjects, view as a very special threat the demand that they change their methods and materials so as to individualize instruction. Traditionally they see themselves as responsible for "covering the course of study" written, for the most part, by department heads or subject committees and handed to them as sacrosanct. Together with the course outline or syllabus, they are given the textbook usually selected from the state-approved list because it "follows the course." They believe that text must be studied by all the pupils. Its format includes questions at the end of each chapter, the answers to which all pupils (even those who cannot read the book) are expected to find in the chapter. This makes it unnecessary for the teacher to formulate his own questions. The tests, which may or may not be made up by the teacher, are on the chapters as they are "covered," so students do well if they can read and can memorize the facts as stated on the printed pages. In many classes the pupil is "failed" unless seven of ten questions are answered correctly. Any deviation from this procedure is regarded as "lowering the standards."

The August 16, 1969 issue of *Saturday Review* contains an article by Peter Schrag in which he reports a conference of educators and students held at the Advanced Administrative Institute of the Harvard Graduate School of Education. In the article, "Gloom at the Top," Mr. Schrag quotes a midwestern deputy superintendent of schools who "confessed that two-thirds of the high schools in his district stink and that the kids are perfectly right to scream about teachers who can't teach, administrators who are inaccessible, and programs from another age."

In discussion of the probability of disruption in the junior and senior high schools in 1969–1970, Schrag says in his book, "Race pot, music, and anger of youth—all the elements are there, and so is business as usual. Six hours a day of incarceration, thirty kids to a class, listening to a drone; guidance counselors advising independence, while teachers sniff the john for smoke; hall passes and after school detentions; phony student councils and pompous principals issuing daily homily. They are masters of the put-down, experts in condescension. . . . 'What they're doing,' says a tough angry man from the Minneapolis schools, 'is killing kids.' "[1]

What do the children say (not all, of course, but a significant number of those who need most)? In the *Harvard Educational Review*, Vol. 39, No. 4, 1969, Robert Coles tells of his conversations with children about "Those Places They Call Schools" . . . "I'd have the teacher be better. She could laugh a lot. . . . Half the time I'm ready to fall asleep and the teacher is just as sleepy. . . . All they want is for us to be quiet and polite and mind them. Then they are glad when school is out and they can get away from here . . . she'll give you something to read and then she'll have to take it away and put it in the cabinet and lock it up . . . and what they teach you, it's enough to make you drowsy, drowsy all day."

Junior and senior high school teachers are frustrated by the presence in their classrooms of boys and girls who cannot or will not read; who refuse to answer questions; who have nothing to say in discussion; who are apathetic or withdrawn or alienated or resentful; who are hostile and disruptive; who most certainly are divorced from the learning process. They, like their younger brothers and sisters, seem not to know how to learn; yet nowhere during the ordinary school day is time spent on developing learning skills other than reading, writing, memorizing, and recalling what is in the textbook—if they have read it. Directly and purposefully teaching these young people *how to read* is rarely attempted by secondary school teachers. Few students are ever involved in inquiry training, in analyzing issues, in thinking in depth, and in solving real social and personal problems of living.

Learning to learn is especially important to the so-called disadvantaged pupils in the secondary schools. In addition to not being able to read, many of those pupils reach the junior high school without having had enough practice in developing skill in planning—alone and with others—in examining values, in questioning, in forecasting consequences, and in evaluating self, others, process, and product. They, like the younger children, often have not identified their own responsibility for getting involved—for doing something about learning. They blame their

[1] *Out of Place in America*, Peter Schrag, Random House, Inc. 1970.

teachers for being uninterested or accuse them of not knowing how to teach.

Secondary school students who have not learned how to learn are often regarded by their teachers as nonlearners—people who have little intelligence and dim futures. Unfortunately many of those pupils accept the schools' evaluation of them as true. They see themselves as unable to learn and behave in accordance with that negative perception of self. The teachers face the job of convincing them that they do, in fact, have the ability to learn, that they have already learned much, and that they can learn more. Sometimes it helps to remind such boys and girls that before they became three years old they learned two of life's most difficult skills—to walk and to talk. This should prove to them that they have the mental capacity to learn language and the nerve and muscle capacity to develop coordination skills needed in playing sports, athletics, and dancing which are basically less complex than the skills needed to stand erect and walk.

In adolescence, as in childhood, learning to learn means using the five senses to discover facts about the physical world, to reawaken curiosity and to develop ability to ask questions, to use all kinds of sources (people, places, things, books, newspapers, T.V., radio) to find the answers to questions, to join others in planning and evaluating, to participate in all kinds of direct learning experiences, and to search for their meanings.

Although many secondary schools are engaged in innovative alterations of room sizes and shapes, teacher responsibilities and student schedules, it will take time before the structures of the school day and the programs are changed. Despite common acceptance of the fact that traditional courses and methods do not meet the learning needs of large numbers of students, most of the boys and girls in school now and for the next decade will probably be expected to sit through traditionally departmentalized programs. Their classrooms will still be boxlike places where learning experiences will consist, for the most part, of listening to teacher lectures and reading the printed pages in traditional and still unrevised textbooks. If all who attend school are to learn, ways must be devised to break through the lockstep methods and materials of mass instruction. Learning centers based upon the principles developed in the foregoing section on elementary schools are one possibility.

It should be possible to create learning centers related to specific subject areas and locate them in or near the rooms, laboratories, or shops used for those courses. For example, a center devoted to learning about the self (see page 30) could be developed in the Home Arts suite and made available to all students of both sexes. This would be a place where they could develop skills in communicating feelings and thoughts, verbally and nonverbally through facial expressions and gestures. These skills are needed in human relations.

Reading, writing, listening, and talking learning centers like those described on pages 32–37 but developed on more mature levels and placed in English classrooms, adjacent corridors, or libraries would help to vitalize language arts programs. Drama centers set up on or behind the auditorium stage would enable many students other than just the select drama club members to use spontaneous dramatics and role-playing to learn the skills and arts of human relations. Literature books read in and out of class and their own social and psychological experiences could furnish the content for the pupils' dramatic adventures.

Look-see learning centers set up in or near Social Studies classrooms would need to be equipped with relevant pictures of the places and peoples being studied, with charts and maps, with the necessary projectors, films, filmstrips, and slides which would enable individuals or small groups to use them for learning in addition to, or instead of, books.

Science teachers always have made more or less use of the five senses to develop powers of observation. They need the equipment which will enable them to shift from teacher demonstration of experiments to individual involvement in doing. Magnifying glasses, microscopes, models, charts, and living specimens need to be supplied in sufficient quantities to enable individuals to work with them. In addition to the laboratory the great outdoors should become the learning center for direct experience with the world. This is especially important for general science and biology courses and for independent learning projects in geology and the study of weather, for example.

Secondary school shops, of course, are direct experience learning centers. However, they need to be opened to all pupils of both sexes and to allow for individual choice of activity and production. In too many places mass production of articles unrelated to the real life of the students continues to dominate. Very often shops are unused for many periods during the day.

Shops, kitchens, sewing rooms, laundries, and small living suites are logically the places to be reconstituted as centers for learning the skills and arts of human relations and for discussing parenthood, the nature of family life, and its implications for the full development of children.

The open secondary school now in experimental operation in a few places is not too difficult to envision in an ordinary situation. If the learning or resource centers are open for use whenever a student wishes to go there, and if it also becomes possible for teachers to take students into the community to learn at first hand about people, places, things, business, industry, the processes of government, and the problems of living in our society, students will become interested and more fully informed than they could be with use of books alone in closed classrooms. If this requires the end of departmentalization as such, so be it. However, if cooperatively planned by several departments— English, Social Studies, Business Education, and Humanities— any trip will provide multiple learning experiences and outcomes in creative discussion and activity.

It is as important for secondary school students to keep learning logs as for the younger children. These present evidence of success in learning to the student himself, to his parents, and to the teacher. As with little children, teachers must learn to recognize and praise every successful learning experience and outcome and to avoid comparison of one pupil's learning with another's especially with respect to quantity. Learning in school is not a competitive sport; the objective is not to pick a winner. When an individual learns as much as he can, he is not a failure. Motivation and effort for learning are increased by success and killed by failure.

At the secondary school level many students will profit if more time is spent learning from people—those at home and in the community as well as those who can be brought into the classroom as speakers and resource persons. Already employed as aides in many schools are people expert in living. Moreover, in every community there are men and women who are retired from the professional, labor, and art fields who would gladly come in to share their experiences and expertise with the youth. Those invited should be from all racial, religious, and ethnic groups in the community and, if the population is homogeneous, from elsewhere. They should be people representing all kinds of earning activities, struggling to solve all types of human relations and social problems, directing all sorts of social and civic agencies, working in all levels of local, state and national government, doing research in science and human welfare. Students must learn how to learn from people—how to plan for interviews, what to ask, how to conduct themselves when presenting their own points of view, and how to differ without anger.

The open school, use of the community for learning, and its special revelance for black students is discussed by Chester Davis in his article "Approaches to Black Education" appearing in the November–December issue of *Integrated Education:* "Students can discover much about the history of their community and of Black people in general simply by talking with, or interviewing some of its elder citizens . . . about family life, migration patterns, occupations, religious life, folklore, organizations, struggles. Many senior Black people [others, too] have historical artifacts, scrapbooks, letters, photographs, lockets, and items of clothing." They know about ". . . Black land ownership after the Reconstruction period, Black artisans and craftsmen, sheriffs and badmen, families, schools and plantations." Davis further cites an example of what happened to "slow learners" and the "unmotivated" in a large Northern city when students undertook investigation of the Underground Railroad. They went to "nearby communities where they interviewed descendents of slaves who had escaped, and visited a house complete with underground tunnels where slaves were hidden. As a result the students and their parents embarked on a reading program."

Davis recommends that "Black students [and indeed all others] could investigate the histories of the institutions, formal groups and societies, churches, clubs, fraternal societies, self-help organizations, newspapers, community centers. They could look into the histories of Blacks [or their own racial or ethnic groups] in the various occupations [lower level, middle level and prestige] such as firemen, police, teachers, skilled craftsmen, business, [science, art, writing and music]."

The importance of these learning experiences lies in the

process and the outcomes in the development of skills, insight, and understanding instead of in the content or facts that are learned; certainly what information is gathered and retained will differ from student to student. There is no doubt that students so involved get practice in reading, writing, listening, reporting, interviewing, research, map and chart making, and interpreting —the tools and skills of the historian.

Secondary school pupils greatly need opportunities to learn about themselves. They and their teachers especially need to understand emotions and behavior related to the developmental tasks of adolescence, the years characterized by the search for identity. The teen-ager wants to know, "Who am I in relation to parents and other authority figures? Who am I in relation to sex? Who am I in relation to the nation and its government? Who am I in relation to the working world?" These are the years in which the youngster wants to be recognized as an adult, to make his own decisions, to move out from under the domination of the father. However, when the decisions they do make differ from those the adult would prefer, conflict begins.

Rebellion against authority, demonstrations of dissent, and protests against adult values and behavior patterns with which secondary school students are preoccupied are often deplored, punished, or ignored by teachers; yet they constitute the realities of life and so must find a place in the school's curriculum. Until the young people have the understanding and skills they need to cope with themselves, others, and the environment, they are likely to be unwilling to give their time and attention to courses of study concerned with matters seemingly remote in time and space and unrelated to their own lives.

The other developmental task which creates problems for teen-agers and their teachers is adjustment to sex and sex relations. Teachers are aware of the conditions which make sex an open book for children at an early age in poverty stricken homes; yet some of them regard this as an indication of what they call "lower moral standards" on the basis of which they tend to reject the student and his parents. Sex knowledge and experimentation are certainly not limited to the poor nor does the fact that some pupils are more sophisticated in this regard preclude the general need for opportunities to discuss the facts of life and the values which direct choice of alternative behaviors in relation to parenthood, early marriage, and the effects of family structure on the development of children.

Discussion of sex-related problems can take place in English classes where human relations are portrayed in the novels and plays students read in and out of school. They can also be discussed in Social Studies classes where the curriculum is supposed to include study of the serious social issues that confront our society. Family breakdown and overpopulation are among those issues. Surely Health Education is incomplete without sex hygiene. General Science and Biology cannot omit reproduction.

Throughout the secondary school, no matter what the subject may be, the emphasis needs to be shifted from teaching to learning. What matters most is not what a teacher teaches but what a pupil learns. If these students can learn how to learn before they graduate, they will have no difficulty succeeding in institutions of higher education. The learning centers are of paramount importance as places where heavy emphasis can be placed on the skills of learning. Whether the center is in the shop, the laboratory, the classroom, the library, the community or the countryside, pupils can be expected to learn from people, things, places, pictures, and eventually from books when they know that all five senses are to be used in the learning process.

7 ADAPTING TO INDIVIDUAL DIFFERENCES

"Individualized instruction will become a necessity rather than a luxury. Because of the great number of people to be taught, the great variety in their backgrounds, and finally, the necessity to provide instruction when the learner needs it, the traditional class and classroom model will have to be replaced. The learner must be able to begin when the need occurs and at the place and pace most appropriate for him."

John W. Loughary
"Educating for Humaneness in the Technological Society," Chapter 10
Association for Supervision and Curriculum Development,
To Nurture Humaneness, Yearbook 1970

The following rather simplified method for recognizing and accepting individual differences may seem to apply more to elementary than to secondary schools. However, it does work at all levels to solve some very common problems caused by differences among the pupils in every classroom.

There comes a time when the teacher who has taught something new (or reviewed a previous lesson) feels that the pupils (or at least many of them) are ready to find out for themselves (and demonstrate to him) whether or not they have learned what he has taught. If the lesson has been arithmetic, he says, "Now take out your arithmetic books"; if history, his order is "Turn to the questions at the end of the chapter"; if English "Open the grammar book."

It is not uncommon at this point for teachers to wait until all the books are out and ready for use before giving further directions. Time is wasted because people differ in the speed with which they attack any job. Some have an inner drive to get to work, some have to be driven. People who have a fast reaction time get to work at once; those who at all times react slowly need an interval in which to gather themselves together. Some students are habitually without books, paper, and pencils and must get them from the teacher or classmates. Others simply require physical movement to ease stretched muscles, so they walk to the sharpener to get new points on broken or unbroken pencils. All this time those who are ready and anxious to get going have nothing to do. They become bored and restless, begin to talk to neighbors, and in other ways disrupt the class.

The procedure can easily be changed. Instead of saying, "Take out your books," the teacher may better say, "When you are ready to find out whether or not you have learned what I have been teaching (explaining or showing) you how to do, you will find sentences (or problems or questions) on page 00." He immediately writes this number on the board. He may, at the same time, tell and write the number of the question or problem with which the pupils are to begin.

When the teacher puts these numbers on the board, he is recognizing individual differences in his students' ability to pay attention, to hear, and to remember. This simple act prevents the annoyance of waving hands and asking either the teacher or others, "What did he say?" As soon as he writes the page on the board, the teacher must say loudly and clearly, **"Do as many as you can."** With this simple order the teacher recognizes and acknowledges to his class that he knows they differ in developmental levels, skills, styles of learning, and work habits. He accepts the fact that the pupils differ from each other in motivation, energy level, rate and amount of learning and of production.

When the students know that the quality of their work is more important than the quantity, they are released from the pressure of time. (There may be other occasions when time becomes a factor to be considered.) When students find themselves accepted even if they learn or produce slowly, the teacher is no longer a threat. When they know that no one will be compared with another and looked down on by his peers because he learns more slowly than they do or has not yet developed the required skills, he is not plagued by the stress and strain of unfair competition. When he knows he will not be called a failure because he did not learn the first time around or is not yet ready for a particular task, he does not become unbearably anxious. At the same time, the order, **"Do as many as you can,"** retains the atmosphere of challenge for the fast learner who cannot finish, become bored, restless, talkative, and unhappy.

"Do as many as you can" is both simple and complex. It does not mean the same if "can" is replaced by "want to" or "would like to do"—phrases so often used by mistaken teachers. When properly stated and emphasized it helps to prevent such blocks to learning as a negative self-image, a high anxiety level, and the threat of losing the race or failing again. It helps teachers to determine which pupils learn quickly, which ones need a second (or a third) go around, which ones need individual help, and which few are not yet ready for the task at hand. It challenges the rapid learners and solves some of their behavior problems. It helps the teacher to move from mass instruction toward individualization.

READING

Students above the primary level who read below grade level present upper elementary and secondary school teachers with their most difficult problem. Teachers who are liberal arts graduates may have had no opportunity to experience or study methods of instruction other than lectures. They tend to be angry whenever a speaker or supervisor says, "Every teacher must teach reading." The following suggestions are not offered as a panacea to solve all reading problems but rather to give inexperienced teachers some clues about teaching older children and adolescents how to read.

Before a student can read a page or a paragraph or even a sentence, he must have a degree of familiarity with the words in it. Therefore the first step is to ask him to point out the words he does not know. In any heterogeneous class some pupils will know most of the words; some will know only a few. At once subgrouping, perhaps better described as arranging pupils for instructional purposes, becomes essential. The able readers can proceed on their own and at their own desks, using dictionaries to find pronunciations and meanings.

The rest of the class can then be divided (or arranged in) small groups depending on the degree of reading skills. If the room has tables, the teacher will want to assemble the least able readers around one at which he is seated. It should be within reach of the chalk board or an easel equipped with a large tablet. The next one or two groups can be around tables or can bring their desks into circles. These groups can be led by teacher aides or able pupils. The process for identification of unknown words is the same. In each case the teacher or leader must assist the pupils to decode each unknown word, to sound it out, to say it, and to deduce its meaning from its prefix, suffix, and root. At the lowest reading level, once the word study is complete, the teacher will probably find it advisable to read the passage to the group while they follow in their books. Then they should read silently, more than once if necessary, until they have developed some degree of fluency and can comfortably read it aloud. The leader can then test comprehension of the passage by asking questions.

The material used to teach secondary school students how to read must not insult their intelligence. Primers and first grade or even third grade readers are out of the question. Local newspapers, some pamphlets and magazines and most advertising materials are on low reading levels and can be used. In some situations having the students create their own textbooks produces good results. This is often referred to as the "experience chart" method. Teachers who plan to use it should see it in operation in any first grade classroom. The content and language, of course, will be quite different from what should be used at an upper grade level.

The method begins with an experience. If this is not feasible, a prior experience that all the pupils in the subgroup can recall, will do. One day an English teacher who planned to combine reading with group writing struck a match and asked the class to observe all they could, to describe their sensations of sight, sound and smell, and then to create a story of events that could follow. Those who could proceeded with the task. The teacher gathered those he wanted to teach around a table and used the following method:

He asked a student in the group to tell one thing he remembered about the experience and wrote that statement on a large tablet standing on a nearby easel. He then asked the student to read it; then the whole group to read it together. Each student in the group added another memory which the teacher wrote, the student read, the group read. So the process continued until memories were exhausted and creative group-writing had been achieved. When the writing and reading were finished, the students copied their creation into their own English notebooks.

In some subject areas such writings could become a textbook for these pupils.

This kind of reading-writing experience will be of interest and value to students and teacher if it has to do with their personal lives, feelings, hopes, worries, problems, and intentions. It should give them a chance to talk and read about their frustrations and anger, to raise questions they need to get answered, to put into words their doubts and fears. The teacher can universalize these problems by reading to them poetry and prose selections that deal with similar people and events the world over.

Direct and immediate sensory experiences will be most effective in stimulating thoughts. For example, five or ten minutes directed observation outside the building or at an open window can generate thoughts and questions about the weather, the soil, or some aspects of the plant and animal life in the region. The pupils can be asked to note what air smells like before, during, and after rain or snow; how the body reacts to wind, to cold, to heat of the sun; how rain or sleet feels on the face; how it feels to walk on grass, concrete, or a pebbled road. All of this will be more effective in a science class than an attempt to use a textbook with pupils who cannot read. While retarded readers are having an experience and then telling-reading-writing about it, others in the class can be engaged in independent learning projects, in studying the textbook, or in working with microscopes, models, and charts.

Creative and imaginative speaking and writing together with recall can be initiated by having pupils shake hands with each other, remember the face of a friend, relive a funny experience. Looking out the window can provide fresh experiences: clouds; a bird in flight; a bird pecking for food; leaves on the trees; leaves falling to earth in a late fall windstorm; a man at work; cars driving by; huge machines doing work while men stand by idle.

Although teachers have long known that it is not true, most of them across the nation teach incoming classes as if promotion from one grade to another means that, because students have approximately the same chronological age, they have attained similar levels of development, have acquired the same amount of information, remember the same amounts of it, and are equally skilled in doing both mental and physical things. When they inevitably find that the students differ in all those respects, they tend to blame previous teachers, especially first grade teachers. Many teachers assume that if they "teach hard enough" and "the pupils will only work harder," all of them will "catch up by the end of the year." They then proceed to teach as if this result can be accomplished by giving all the students the same work to do and a "little more help to those who are having a hard time keeping up." Mass instruction continues to dominate the classrooms of the secondary schools.

The teachers do know, of course, that rates of learning and production vary widely in every classroom; therefore, since they are sensitive to the needs of the slow learners, they pace instruction slowly. They then close their eyes to evidence of boredom shown by the more rapid learners yet express concern about "holding them back." They say they "teach to the dullest at the expense of the brightest," and both they and parents worry about "lowering standards."

Supervisors and consultants are confronted with the question, "How can we, ordinary classroom teachers, provide for a wide range of reading levels, developmental levels, and learning styles and still keep the class together?" The following examples of classroom instruction in several different subject areas include descriptions of methods of teaching by mass instruction and of moving toward individualization, and of providing for individual differences without disrupting the class, removing pupils from it, or using elaborate and expensive machines. The suggestions are based on valid general principles of learning. Although they deal with specific subjects and maturity levels, they can be adapted to other subjects and grades.

LESSON ASSIGNMENT IN SOCIAL STUDIES #1
Undifferentiated Mass Instruction

The period was almost over. In fact, most of the students had already stacked their books on their desks and were ready to leap out of their seats as soon as the bell rang. Many were talking to neighbors. Mr. Smith, the teacher, rapped smartly on the table with his ruler to get some degree of attention. "I forgot to give you your assignment," he said. "For tomorrow I want you all to study Chapter 10 in your textbook. It is about political parties. Get the answers to the questions at the end of the chapter, if you can. I may give you a test on them before we have discussion." The bell rang and in a few minutes the room was empty.

Did Mr. Smith assume that everyone heard the assignment? Was he under the impression that everyone in the class could read the textbook? He obviously doubted that all the students could get the answers to the questions and by saying "if you can" indicated that he expected some pupils to do poorly the next day. (Evidence is accumulating that teachers get from pupils approximately what they expect to get.) The only motivation that Mr. Smith provided for doing the assignment was a vague threat to "give a test" on the questions before discussing them. Giving a test implies getting a mark; the teacher holds this out as the main reason for doing the work.

LESSON ASSIGNMENT #2
Providing for Individual Differences

The class had been engaged in a study of politics instigated by local elections. Mr. Walters, the teacher, feeling that the work under way had reached the point at which to make a new assignment, called the class to attention. He said, "You need to know something more about political parties. Several questions were raised today which Jerry wrote on the side board. Please read them over and then we will consider others that should be added. Martha will you write them on the board, please, and all of you copy them in your notebooks to guide you in your search for information. (This is a good example of pupil participation in determining content.) Get as much information about as many of the questions as you can. You will have class time to work as well as the weekend. The first discussion will be scheduled for Monday.

"Since I expect everyone to contribute to the discussions," Mr. Walters continued, "we had better take time now to decide where the information can be obtained and who is to be primarily responsible for consulting each source. By the way, what sources are there?" Without the formality of raising hands, individuals called out, "Encyclopedias"; "Reference books"; "The text"; "Supplementary books in the closet"; "Newspapers"; "Radio"; "Television." "You forgot people," Mr. Walters offered. "Now," he continued, "I would like to make sure we do get information from all those sources, so let me make some assignments. Sally, Jim, and Bill will you concentrate on people. Interview your parents; ask the storekeepers in the neighborhood; talk to your friends and to other adults." These were pupils who, Mr. Walters knew, had reading difficulties.

The assignment continued: "Joan, Carl, and Sue (all able readers and good students) will you consult the encyclopedias and reference books in the library. Here is the list. The librarian has it too and has already placed these titles on the reserve shelf. You can also get them checked out in the public library for use at home."

Next, calling the names of several boys and girls who, as Mr. Walters knew, were more ear than eye minded, he handed them the current radio and TV schedules and reminded them to watch for new ones on the weekend and to decide among themselves for which newscasts each would be responsible. He was careful not to include in this group anyone to whom, because of poverty, radio and TV sets were not likely to be available.

The next subgroup of three or four pupils were those who had no trouble using the regular classroom text and supplementary books. He reminded them that they could check these out for home use especially on the weekend.

Four pupils, not quite on grade reading level, were asked to use the newspapers. (Daily papers usually run from sixth to eighth grade levels). Mr. Walters reminded this group that the daily papers including the New York Times (although he knew the level was higher than most) were available in the library. He also said that back issues and papers from other places would be valuable and that these could be used in the public library.

Finally Mr. Walters suggested that many of the group would find the questions interesting for dining and living room conversations, so getting information from people was not to be limited to Sally, Bill, and Jim. He also suggested that "everyone was free to use radio and TV and newspapers and, indeed, any other source of information available to them."

Mr. Walters' plan for the discussion was first to organize conversation circles in which pupils assigned to the various sources would be mixed up. This would provide opportunities for successful contribution from all pupils. Before they disbanded, he expected to ask each circle to formulate one unanswered question to place before the entire class when discussion was resumed on the following day.

AN ENGLISH CLASS #1
Mass Instruction

The class was engaged in vocabulary building and sentence structure. The teacher, Mrs. Stevens, said to the entire group, "Write two sentences using six words in each. Try to use the words from the geography lesson." Some of the pupils had a hard time getting down to that task. A few had pencils to sharpen. Some had no paper. Others did not hear and had to ask neighbors, "What did she say?" Eventually all was quiet, but by then several had finished their sentences and had nothing further to do. One of them sat quietly dreaming; another started to talk to a neighbor; several began to tap their pencils; still another got up and walked around the room. As others finished their work the noise and disturbance grew. The teacher stood silently at the rear of the room, glanced around from time to time, and waited for the slowest child to put his pencil down.

At last all seemed to be ready for the next step. Mrs. Stevens said, "Who wants to put their sentence on the board?" A few hands were raised and six children were selected who walked slowly up to the front boards. There, with more or less erasing and rewriting, in handwriting more or less legible, they each wrote one short sentence. During this slow and somewhat painful process all the other pupils waited with nothing to do.

When the children at the boards were finished, the teacher asked each in turn to read the sentence to the class. She then turned to the group and said, "Does anyone see something wrong?" Hands went up and a child was picked to go correct a misspelled word or change a punctuation mark or alter the number of a noun or the tense of a verb. Most of the pupils in the class were uninvolved. The teacher used no terms of evaluation except to say at every possible moment, "all right" or "OK." No mention was made of what the sentences said. No credit was given for truth or beauty or originality.

AN ENGLISH CLASS #2
Providing for Individual Differences

Paper and pencils were provided for those who had none, and everyone was ready for work. The teacher, Mrs. Martin, said, "You have been working on sentences, so it is now time to see how well you have learned. What are the various kinds that you can use?" From around the room, without the formality of raising hands and without shouting, came the answers, "Complex"; "Simple"; "Compound." "Very good, indeed," said the teacher. "Now, in the next ten minutes, each one please write *as many sentences as you can,* and in each sentence use a different number of words. Remember the time is short." No limit was placed on quantity so no one could finish and have nothing to do. The word *can* implied a challenge and also showed that the teacher expected different pupils to do a different amount of work.

When ten minutes had passed, Mrs. Martin called time and asked the children to put down their pencils. She then said, "I would like to have some of you put your sentences on the board so we can look at them." Immediately hands went up, but the teacher selected a dozen pupils including some who had not raised their hands. Her choice was made on the basis of what she knew about the differences in her pupils' abilities to handle language. She wanted a variety of sentences, and she wanted some who could write only short simple sentences to have the experience of being chosen.

While the students were working at the boards, Mrs. Martin called upon many individuals in the class to read their sentences—usually limiting each child to the one the child thought to be his best. Again she included all levels of ability. She greeted each child's effort warmly and used many words of evaluation—never once saying merely, "all right" or "OK." She also gave the class an opportunity to reward those who participated. Sometimes this was in words, sometimes children gave one clap. Praise did not depend upon the number of words used or the complexity of the sentence but rather on what it said—on its truth or beauty or originality.

As soon as the children working at the board were back in their places, the teacher asked each in turn to read the sentence to the class. When a correction was suggested by a classmate, Mrs. Martin called upon others to agree or disagree. Emphasis was always placed on correctness and content. Very few pupils did not take part in the work. Mrs. Martin brought them in by calling upon them individually to read a sentence to the class. Then she asked if anyone else had a sentence he or she wanted very much for the class to hear. Some children responded and the lesson was over. In addition to giving the children a chance to participate orally and in writing, Mrs. Martin had looked at many children's work as she moved around the room during the period. No child could possibly leave that room feeling ignored by the teacher or rejected by classmates.

CREATIVE WRITING

What can be done about creative writing when some of the class can't write a complete sentence while others write material worthy of publication?

Creative writing or English composition is a responsibility shared by elementary and secondary school teachers. In junior high schools it may be part of the language-arts course or units of work in block-of-time classes or Core—a term used in many states such as North Carolina, Michigan, Kentucky, and Arkansas. In senior high school it may be in the regular required English classes, in journalism or in advanced composition electives. The following methods of providing for a range of abilities and skills can be adapted to all grade levels.

In the simplest method most frequently used, the teacher assigns a topic, a subject, or an opening sentence to the entire class. For example, a recently observed teacher required a whole class to write a composition about *one* thing each would take along on a trip to outer space! The "lesson" begins with a warm-up conversation to stimulate ideas and create enthusiasm for a subject which the teacher believes will appeal to all the pupils. There are few such subjects, however. The assignment may have no interest for some because they have had little or no related background experiences. In all probability there will also be others who have not developed the thought or the language skills required, and some who cannot write; as a result many pupils will remain uninvolved. Usually teachers include in the preparation for writing reminders of grammatical elements and format which they expect to take into account when they mark the papers. Too often they neglect emphasis on such elements as truth, beauty, and originality.

It is obvious, then, that a mass assignment will not be suitable. The teacher who has in mind the wide range of differences that exist in any class opens the discussion by saying something like, "There are many things you might consider writing about today. Everyone in the class may have his own choice of subject. If you will tell us, I will put a list of your ideas on the board." He then writes "Options" and lists *everything* offered by members of the class. When all who want to have responded, he adds the word "Others" in order to leave the door open for any who were reluctant to tell the class what they were thinking about.

At this point pupils need time to explore the meaning of some suggested subjects, to ask questions about suitability, and to get a look at unfamiliar words and expressions that would be helpful. The teacher writes these on the board as they come up, helps the pupils to analyze them, to decode, to read. If this help is not needed by some, they may want to begin at once to write and, in order to give the necessary concentration, may request permission to move their desks into the corridor or go to the library.

In addition to individual choice of topic, students may be given choice of writing alone, in pairs, or in groups of three or four. At other times the teacher may make the decision and ask all to rearrange themselves in small groups to experience group writing or he may require each to work entirely alone.

There are times when topic sentences given by the teacher or members of the class are "open end"—related to personal thoughts and experiences. Students must be assured that these will be read only by the teacher himself and that they will not have to share them with classmates and that the teacher will not show them to another teacher or counselor or principal. Such topics, however, often produce good writing as well as information and insight the teacher needs concerning the life style, problems, needs, hopes and desires of individual boys and girls. Another device that produces good results when ideas are slow in coming or it seems difficult for some to get started is to tell pupils to begin with a sentence or word that comes to mind and keep writing without stopping to even think for ten minutes. This stream of consciousness writing is often most interesting to students and their teachers.

Finally the writing time begins and no limits are set for finishing. The teacher's challenge is, "Write as much as you can now. You may want to finish at home, but we will return to this tomorrow." Some students will be ready to get to work at once and to work steadily. Not everyone can do that when faced with a creative job. They will need time to think or dream or move around. Some people are accustomed to write first and correct afterwards; others correct and rewrite as they go.

Now the teacher is ready to carry out his plan for those in the class who cannot write. His objective is to give them a success experience in creative thinking and group writing and, at the same time, to increase their skill in reading. He calls these pupils by name asking them to join him at a table placed within reach of the chalkboard. If he fears this will call too much attention to what he is doing and for whom, he may place himself and them at the rear of the room and use an easel with a large pad of newsprint paper for his writing.

First, members of this subgroup must be given time to agree on a topic. If those on the board have no appeal, it may be necessary to provide an immediate experience to write about. For example, they might look out the window and talk about what they see. They may watch their classmates at work for a few minutes and discuss their observations. They might be interested in describing each other's faces or personalities. The teacher may offer a provocative picture or have the group listen to a radio commercial or watch a part of a soap opera on T.V. and try to write the next episode.

When the pupils are ready to begin writing, the teacher asks one for an opening statement which he writes on the tablet or the chalkboard. The procedure is that described as experience reading on page 52.

At the end of the writing period or on the following day, students should have time to read their creations to their classmates. Some will be able to do so for the whole class. Others will be too timid or diffident or threatened to talk before so large a group. For their sake, and in order to quadruple the number who will have an opportunity for sharing, small mixed circles can be arranged for the purpose. Those students who worked with the teacher should read their product to classmates and be praised as all others are, especially for truth, beauty, and originality. Thus praise and success can be experienced by all members of the class.

Arrangements for a group writing and reading experience for the least able pupils does not fulfill the teacher's responsibility to help others in the class. He may need to sit down with a student and help him write his first sentence or write for him a list of words he will need. Instead of doing this himself, from time to time the teacher should ask able students to act as teacher-aides instead of writing. Some students are able to accept help from their peers more readily than from their teachers.

Students who have much ability to write should be challenged to write as often and as much as they can about anything. Perhaps they should record their thoughts and observations every day. No due dates or time limits should be set for them. Each one should file his work in his own folder to be read at the teacher's convenience. The teacher will then want to have individual conferences with these students to criticize their work and to help them to polish it for possible publication in the school or local newspapers. The object of this writing should always be quality rather than quantity, content rather than grammar and format, personal improvement rather than marks.

Able writers should also be given outlets and incentives for using their talents in the service of others. Thus they should become the class and club secretaries to keep minutes of proceedings and daily journals. They should also have opportunity to practice leadership skills by acting as the leaders when group writing is done. Their regular responsibilities can include writing letters of invitation and thanks to speakers and resource persons who come to address the student body or work with a classroom group. They are the ones who should be called upon to write skits and plays for assembly programs and scripts for radio or T.V. broadcasts.

Piaget reminds us that if the discrepancy between what the child knows and what the environment offers him is just large enough, the result is pleasure; if too large, the result is distress; if none, the result is boredom.

TEACHING MATHEMATICS #1
Mass Instruction

This was, to use the Principal's terminology, the lowest seventh-grade Arithmetic class. It consisted of seventeen pupils, eleven of whom were boys; ten of the boys were nonwhite; four of the six girls were nonwhite. The teacher, Mrs. Roberts, had told the class to open their books to page twenty and do the first ten examples. The pupils were seated in an irregular fashion around the room, but most were near the windows. Some of the girls had erected barricades of pocketbooks and school books behind which they presumably were doing the assignment. The teacher was seated at her own desk in the front of the room where she had buried her attention in some clerical or other work.

Inspection of what the pupils were actually doing revealed that those behind the barricades were not doing arithmetic. They did not know how to do the simple computations required in the examples. What they needed and were not getting was work with concrete materials to establish number concepts.

More that half of the other pupils who were trying to do the assignment, were making mistakes that, with a little individual help, they would be able to understand and correct. The remainder of the boys and girls were succeeding well; two had completed the task and had nothing else to occupy their time.

TEACHING MATHEMATICS #2
Providing for Individual Needs Through Grouping and the Use of Student Aides

The teacher, Miss Clarke, believed that anything new should be presented to the entire class whether or not all the students were ready for it. She said, "You never know when someone can make a sudden leap forward and also I don't want anyone to feel left out or prevented from learning if he can." She therefore taught a new lesson from the chalkboard, went over the process thoroughly, had pupils participate in the calculations when they could, and gave as much time as necessary to the questions individuals asked. Then, feeling that she had done all that was required, she said, "Take out your books, open to page 65 [which she wrote on the board], begin with example 4 [which she added on the board] and *do as many as you can.*"

Miss Clarke went at once to the left front part of the room where she said to four pupils, "Pull your desks around into a circle, I have something special for you to do this period. She handed each a mimeographed sheet of directions and then brought from a nearby table concrete materials—an abacus, some cut out forms, some paper money, cuisenaire rods, and number combination flash cards. She then sat down with them and in a low voice explained and answered their questions. Obviously these were pupils who did not know the fundamentals.

As soon as this group was at work, Miss Clarke went quickly to the other side of the room where she had concentrated what she termed her "second-go-arounds." The students pulled their desks into a circle and she again sat down and, saving her voice, went over the entire process she had taught to the class. Questions were raised and answered and work in this circle continued.

By this time, Miss Clarke knew that her "Whiz Kids" would be ready to show her that they had command of the new work. They were at the rear of the room. She went to them, reached for their papers, saw that they knew what they were doing and said, "I believe you are ready to be my assistants. Mary, will you watch the left side for hands; John, take the right side; Sue, take the middle. If you find something you cannot handle give me a signal, and I will come to that pupil at once. Peter and Sam, I will need you up front."

Miss Clarke then returned to the "fundamentalers." She saw their need, called Peter, told him what was going on and what to do, listened for a few minutes and then went to the "second-go-arounds." There one or two were all right, but the others needed help. Sam was called in and at once began to work with one boy. Miss Clarke sat down to work with one girl, while keeping an eye on her aides for distress signals.

TEACHING SCIENCE

Individualization of instruction in the science classroom should be easier than in most subjects. However, the science teacher echoes the others when he asks, "But how can I possibly teach

Biology to a class in which most of the pupils can't re
books that I have to use for this course?" This sou
indeed when it comes from one specialized in an
depends so much upon observation and direct senso
for the collection of information about the living world.

Where teachers are permitted to do so in the many, many
schools situated handsomely on large tracts of land, Biology
classes should spend a considerable amount of time outside the
building studying plant and animal life at first hand. (Obviously,
in the city school "fresh" materials must be brought into the
classroom by the teacher and the pupils.) Both outside and inside
the classroom, individuals should have freedom to examine
those things that interest them most. All need not look for or
look at the same things at the same time. One thing they should
learn to know, to enjoy, and to value is nature's great diversity.

When the class is resumed after direct experience, the teacher
cannot expect all the students to have seen and learned the same
facts or to have made the same number of observations. If diversity in learning from direct sensory experience is inevitable,
then the teacher must provide diverse materials for students to
use to verify their observations and to extend their learnings.
Those who can read should find relevant books in the room and
the library. Many science books for children and adults are very
well illustrated. These should be provided for pupils who are
eye-minded, who can learn readily from pictures what they cannot get from word symbols. Every well equipped science room will
have charts, specimens, models, magnifying glasses, and microscopes all of which are sources of information that can be used
by students who have reading difficulties but who like to handle
things.

While most of the class are working with books, pictures,
models and specimens, the teacher can meet with that small number of boys and girls who need reading instruction. As they
describe what they saw, he writes down what they say; they read
what he writes (having just said it); they copy the statements in
their notebooks; thus they write and learn to read their own
books which deal directly with whatever aspect of plant or
animal life they are studying. If secondary school teachers have
had no experience with this method of using "experience charts"

to teach reading, they should be given opportunities to observe it in use in elementary schools, or supervisors should demonstrate it for them.

The variety of sources used by students may encourage them to use various ways of expressing their learnings. The teacher should not expect those with reading difficulties to write descriptive answers to test questions or to check answers or fill in blank spaces on objective tests which they cannot read. In some cases a well constructed and labeled chart, or diagram may show how much a student has learned. A clay model of a plant or an insect or an animal skeleton would show quite adequately what a student knows about its body structure. Original drawings or paintings may be the best way for some pupils to express how they feel about the unit and what they have learned.

When diversity of abilities is recognized and instruction is in terms of individual skills and development, competition for marks is not likely to dominate the classroom. The teacher will be unable to evaluate students' learnings on the basis of comparative and standardized test marks but rather will look for evidence of individual growth.

TEACHER AIDES

Individualization of instruction is easier to accomplish if more than one person is accessible to pupils in the ordinary classroom. Although the teacher's need for assistance has been widely recognized by school officials, there are no uniform answers to such questions as: how are aides to be secured; what criteria should be used in hiring them; what training must be provided and by whom; what are they to do in the classroom? One serious obstacle to development of aide programs has been lack of money to pay them. Discussion of only one of those questions is appropriate in the context of this book—what can aides do to help the teacher accomplish individualization of instruction?

Teachers and administrators commonly agree that aides should not do initial instruction. That must remain the responsibility of the professional teacher. In the usual classroom, however, after the teacher has presented new instruction to the entire group, the pupils then either practice or meet in subgroups to discuss the subject that has just been presented. The aide then can help children. The follow-up discussion groups will need someone to answer individual questions, to raise questions for which pupils need to seek answers, and to explain matters that are not yet understood. If the mass instruction is followed by individual seat work, the aide can quickly find pupils who are completely at sea and help them to get started, thus preventing them from becoming frustrated or discouraged. She can also find pupils who are making serious mistakes which by repetition may become habits that resist correction.[1]

An example of the need for early discovery and correction occurred in a first grade classroom. The teacher taught the class how to print "E" and "e." She used the overhead projector and the chalkboard, printing the letters over and over while describing what she was doing. The children merely watched her work (they could and indeed should have been doing the same on their own practice papers). Finally the teacher told the pupils to get to work on their practice papers. After a while she began to walk around the room to see what the children were doing. By the time she reached Jimmy, he had a paper full of " Ǝ 's" and "ɘ's." If an aide had been there and had known Jimmy's difficulty in copying letters, she could have taken his hand and have helped him to trace the correct forms and to learn at once how to make the letters correctly.

Teacher aides are invaluable in teaching reading to pupils of all ages, but especially to those who have not learned to read by the time they reach grade three. Remedial reading is most successful when it is done in a one-to-one relationship. Many schools have found it relatively easy to secure tutors for children who cannot learn to read in the classroom situation. In some districts community women have volunteered for this activity. In others they are secured and organized by the PTA. In some places social organizations like the Junior League or church groups become involved.

One of the most successful programs observed was in a school in Winston-Salem/Forsyth County, North Carolina. Every day some fifteen or twenty women reported to the school where each one spent from one to three hours working mostly with individual children. The highly ingenious and creative

[1] For further reference see Noar, Gertrude, "Teacher Aides at Work," NEA, 1967.

principal erected study cubicles on the auditorium stage, in the corners of the cafeteria, at the ends of sufficiently spacious corridors, or on large enough stair landings—wherever space permitted. Each cubicle, walled off by 9 x 12 ft. plywood boards, was equipped with a small table and two or three chairs. Not only did the children in the program learn to read, but there were also large side benefits. Race relations were improved when tutor and pupil differed in that respect. Affluent women became sensitive to the needs of children on welfare and found it possible to help them and their families to solve some of their problems of living. Tutors met with their pupils' parents and helped them to understand their children's learning difficulties. Teachers met with the tutors and gained new insights into what makes children tick. Inevitably as the women discussed their tutoring project with their friends and associates in church and social groups, they acted as interpreters of the school's programs and problems, thus becoming excellent public relations resources for the principal.

ONE-TO-ONE RELATIONSHIPS

Individualization of instruction requires the teacher to define the various levels of development and achievement in the group of pupils, to diagnose the blocks to learning that exist for individuals, and to plan each day's teaching and learning activities in terms of individual learning needs. Teachers are often frightened by the thought that this means they must give each child personal instruction every day—a task far too large to accomplish in view of the ordinary size of elementary classes and the enormous pupil load carried by secondary teachers. Nevertheless, each child must get help if and when he needs it. Recognition of the importance of one-to-one relationships for pupils with learning difficulties has led to the growing use of paraprofessionals (who may be adults or college students), parent volunteers, the pairing of classmates, and cross-age helpers' projects.

Tutoring projects are also under way in many communities in which out of school help is provided by high school and college students who work with children after school hours, on week ends, and during summer vacations. Two important aspects of this kind of individualization of instruction are the continuity of relationship it affords for a child and the absence of threat which many slow learners experience from the authoritative teacher when the classroom setting is more or less dominated by the fear of failure. Part of the success of individual tutoring comes from the pupil's feeling that someone really cares whether or not he does learn. So many "disadvantaged" and minority group pupils are convinced that their school teachers are not interested in them, see no future for them, and believe that they cannot learn.

USE OF MECHANICAL DEVICES

Teaching machines of all kinds have been made available in recent years, especially to teachers of economically disadvantaged pupils. Many teachers, however, have yet to make use of them for individualizing instruction. Machines to increase eye span and reading speed are usually part of the new, though not yet common, language laboratories, but they could be used just as well in regular classrooms if teachers were willing to part with mass instruction. Individual slide viewers, film strip projectors, tapes and records should be available to pupils who learn more readily from pictures and spoken words than from the printed page.

Many textbooks and elementary reading books now include self-correcting programmed material from which individuals can learn at their own rates—if they can read. For many years teachers have also used mimeographed sets of questions and directions for study which provide for minimum and maximum accomplishments to be graded or marked accordingly. These are sometimes called "contracts" for which the pupils are "paid" by receiving marks—a rather dangerous concept which interferes with teaching children that learning has inherent values and is done by the individual for himself, for his own improvement and advancement.

GROUPING

Although school administrators frown upon ability grouping by classes, teachers tend to want to divide pupils among themselves according to "levels of ability" in skill subjects and to prefer to keep them that way for all their academic work. Many teachers are sure that this is the only way they can provide learning experiences for pupils who differ widely in their developmental levels and learning styles. These groups become "tracks" into which pupils are placed for all their classes and from which few are able to escape. Tracking is especially undesirable in desegregated schools for it defeats the schools' responsibility for full development of each and every child's unknown potentialities.

Placement of students in ability tracks is usually determined on the basis of certain criteria, one of which is I.Q. score determined by a group intelligence test. First, research indicates that this score reflects as few as six or eight of the more than 120 elements which psychologists claim to have identified as part of the complex called intelligence. Second, those tests favor middle class pupils in both language and situational contents. Third, teachers do not have the special training and diagnostic sensitivity required for intelligent and responsible use of those tests. Fourth, few teachers ever get the chance to analyze the test papers and therefore get no clues regarding the individual's strength and weakness which need to be known for individualization of instruction purposes. They merely record the scores returned to them by research departments or counselors.

The second criterion used for class placement is the marks recorded by previous teachers. The lack of validity of teachers' marks as indications of what a child knows, the possibility of his development, the kind of situation in which he is most likely to learn will be fully discussed in Chapter 8. It is important to note here, however, that marks are affected by teachers' likes and dislikes and by their expectations of the child's future about which nothing can be predicted for sure.

It is especially important in desegregated schools to realize that racial prejudices and stereotyped thinking about racial characteristics often affect marks given to black children. They are also heavily influenced by behavior which for some pupils may be reaction to the unreality of the school in terms of the child's life or to the restriction of creative impulses which the teacher may neither tolerate nor understand.

A third criterion used in most schools for grouping by ability is the scores on standardized achievement tests. Teachers are especially prone to use these as indications of ability in relation to other children of the same chronological age and grade level. However, since such tests are administered during the year, they are rarely the determining element. Some schools are now "deploying," that is, regrouping for a period in the day, on the basis of scores on reading tests. The unfortunate element in this practice is that teachers get several "levels" in every class and still must find ways to differentiate materials and provide for individualization of instruction. This method, like others which are supposed to group by ability, inevitably results in lower level classes that are heavily male, heavily lower class, heavily nonwhite and heavily disciplinary. Reading scores are deeply affected by early cultural and economic deprivations.

Chronological age may be the best *single* criterion to use in class organization. Years of experience has shown that an average child placed with his age mates tends to behave as they do, attends more regularly, feels more comfortable and therefore has a greater chance of being successful in learning.

Social class is rarely openly admitted to be one of the criteria used to classify pupils, but it does often influence the person who sorts them out. "Sweet, clean, little girls from up on the hill" are not likely to end up in classes in which many children from "across the tracks" are to be found, even if those little girls cannot read.

Grouping by ability that results in tracking, often for all the years a pupil is in school, has widespread effects on his life. He becomes accustomed to thinking of his intellectual status as superior, mediocre, or inferior. His self-esteem or self-image with respect to learning becomes negative or positive. This is especially so when names or labels are attached to the various groups. A child who is in the group called "Turtles," comes to believe that he is slow and not expected to know the right answers. The "S.A.T.'s" or academically talented group members tend to become overly competitive and snobbish. Black children who may have "inherited" disbelief in their ability to learn and to compete successfully with white age mates become fixed in those beliefs and blocked in learning. Everyone behaves as he perceives himself to be.

Motivation and aspiration are limited by low group placement. Too often teachers are convinced that the children in the low group cannot learn and make little effort to teach them. As a result the children who find themselves in dull and slow-paced classes where most of the work consists of drills and unproductive busywork, make little effort to learn. Moreover, if the teacher is convinced that the pupils are nonlearners, he does not attempt to stimulate them to work toward becoming something or somebody. One such teen-ager, asked why he did not like school said, "They make you a nobody." All teachers are not as yet convinced that employment at all levels is now open to black people. Ability grouping can operate as a control factor in an individual's destiny. No teacher should be allowed to "play God" in a child's life. What these children need most, enrichment, they get the least.

Inspiration ordinarily comes from individuals who are in some way superior to or at least different from a person and who are accepted as role models. A child needs someone to look up to, not only a teacher but also a classmate. For lower class children middle class peers may be more effective teachers of their values, ways of speech, living, and behaving than teachers. The peer group may be more helpful than any adult in creating the desire or drive for social mobility. Age mates are also effective teachers. When a pupil who has greater skill or ability helps one who has trouble in learning to read or figure, both of them are inspired by the act of service and the establishment of a good, productive relationship. When the association is across race, religious or social class lines, prejudice is weakened if not altogether eliminated.

Bruno Bettelheim, Director of the Orthogenic School for Disturbed Children and professor of psychology at Chicago University says, "In order to achieve educationally, many children from impoverished homes need to be challenged and motivated by example. Grouping deprives these children of such stimulation. They are left behind as second class students, a situation which is more likely to create hopelessness than to lessen anxiety."[2]

School segregation has supported belief in black inferiority. In 1954, according to many school superintendents, black schools were actually shortchanged. Moreover, the community, the parents, the children, and even the teachers in them and elsewhere always considered black schools inferior. Again it is important to remember that perception of self determines behavior. The sociologists and psychologists who testified before the Supreme Court in the historic 1954 Decision said in no uncertain terms that separate schools can never be equal; therefore

2 Bettelheim, Bruno, *N.E.A. Journal,* March 1965, "Grouping the Gifted."

cannot provide equality of educational opportunity. Children who all their lives have been segregated cannot at once perform up to their potential and are only further harmed by placement in low ability or so-called "basic" classes.

Many pupils in slow-paced basic classes show all the evidence of boredom. Bettelheim, in an article in School Review, Winter 1961, "The Decision to Fail," says, "If the findings of psycho-analytical investigations of feelings have any validity, feelings of boredom arise as a defense against deep feelings of anxiety." Anxiety is also produced by experiences of rejection and inade-quacy when "the sheep are separated from the goats." Anxiety blocks learning. Thus by the very nature of the child's reactions, placement in a low group deprives him of peace of mind and therefore of equal opportunity to learn.

Teachers want to think of classes arranged on the criteria dis-cussed above as being homogeneous. They use this as their justi-fication for continuing to rely on mass instruction. There is no way to get even a small number of pupils who are alike in de-velopmental levels, learning styles, background experiences, ways of behaving, aspirations, interests, and the host of other factors that create and affect learning. Mass instruction in groups or classes at all grade levels and in all academic subject areas is not good enough. Teachers who are being asked to account for the growth and development of all their pupils must learn to sup-plement it with individualized instruction and diversified learn-ing experiences.

Grouping schemes that result in tracks are especially dangerous for nonwhite lower social class pupils. In the basic classes they hear nothing but their own speech patterns and have little ex-perience with the use of standard English other than what the teacher demands for "passing grades." They also see only those behavior patterns common to people with similar environments. Teachers struggle against too great odds in their endeavors to change these patterns. Examples set by other members of the mixed peer group are needed. Experience and research indicate that lower class black children make great strides in intellectual growth when the environment and associates provided by a racially and socially balanced group permit and encourage it.

Junior and senior high school students placed in low ability tracks take little or no part in activity programs. They say they feel unwanted; they say they dislike their teachers and class-mates. When the day ends they want to get away as fast as they can. If activities such as dances are held at night they are un-likely to attend.

Attendance and retention are decidedly lower in basic classes. Teachers are less inclined to care whether or not these students come and often believe they should leave school as soon as the law allows.

Teachers need to be informed about and sensitive to the causes of learning disabilities and blocks in black and lower social class pupils. Faculty study should include:

—the meaning of the "Negro role" which parents in the past taught their children; the changes in that role concept; the conflicting attitudes toward self and others in which black children are now caught.
—family structures and ways in which the matriarchal family affects adolescent attitudes toward the woman teacher and the girl-centered curriculum and the behavior demands of the middle class school.
—the effect of the absence of a father.
—brain damage causes and effects; pre- and post-natal nutri-tion, childhood diseases, head injuries.
—the risk the black child faces in being too bright or eager or in winning.
—the nature and effects of early economic impoverishment.

All children who are now in school and those who will be need preparation for effective living in a fully integrated society. Anything the school can do must be done to assure every child, no matter how he differs from others, full and equal opportuni-ties to develop all his potentialities. Restrictions suffered in the past cannot be tolerated. Ability grouping was one of them.

Writing in "Dark Ghetto," Kenneth Clark has this to say about grouping: ". . . for once one organizes an educational system where children are placed in tracks or where certain judgments about their ability determine what is done for them or how much they are taught or not taught, the horror is that the results seem to justify the assumption . . . . Those children that are relegated to the inferior groups suffer a sense of self doubt and deep feelings of inferiority which stamp their entire attitude toward school and the learning process. . . . They react negatively, and hostilely and aggressively to the educational process. They hate teachers, they hate schools, they hate anything that seems to impose upon them this denigration."

COMMITTEE WORK

Every movement intended to improve education has left some mark upon educational practices. The core curriculum, for example, which flowered in the 1930s and 1940s, has by no means disappeared especially in the junior high schools. However, it persists mainly as a method of organizing the school day rather than as a method of organizing content and providing learning experiences. Thus a teacher may meet with a class group for more than one period a day in an otherwise fully departmentalized school but is likely to be expected in those blocks of time to teach separate subjects—usually English and social studies or mathematics and science. Supervisors, principals, and directors of instruction say they would like teachers to develop units of instruction that combine subjects or "cut across subject matter lines" or at least correlate their subjects. However, they still issue separate subject courses of study and lists of required textbooks that follow those course outlines or guides. Unless teachers have had preservice or in-service training in methods of developing units of learning, they continue to use traditional methods of mass instruction in the separate subjects for which they are responsible.

In the junior high school and, where they exist, in the middle school the block of time which usually is about two hours long, provides a situation in which individualization of instruction could most readily be accomplished through pupil-teacher planning and small group or committee organization. When the teacher prepares a unit, he must decide the purposes for which groups are to be formed and how the membership of those groups is to be determined. Individualization of instruction will not take place if each subgroup is merely assigned only one part of the total content to be covered. In such a plan there is no differentiation in terms of the difficulty of the subject matter or of pupil differences. The pupils in each committee, whether they are assigned or are given a chance to indicate their desires, are usually expected to work in the same way using the same books or other sources of information. Although the students have more opportunities for interaction and for sharing labor and the teacher does less lecturing, there is little if any individualization based on differences in learning styles and differences in levels of ability and degrees of development.

Committee organization can and should be used to secure individualization of instruction in several different ways. One way is to organize so that each subgroup includes the entire spectrum of reading levels, leaders, followers, eye-minded and ear-minded learners, innovators, creative thinkers, and slow learners. In this case the teacher must be sure that the students understand that there are a variety of ways to learn and a variety of sources of information to be used. He must help them to learn how to pool their findings and how to think of a variety of ways both individuals and the group can express their learnings. During the planning sessions the teacher must also help individuals to make decisions regarding the methods they should use, the sources they should consult and the ways to express themselves, all in terms of their personal levels of ability and development and their own learning styles.

Another way to provide individualization through the use of subgroups within a unit of work, is both to organize the committees and to assign their tasks on the basis of individual differences. Then one committee may consist of the most able readers whose job will be to gather information from encyclopedias and reference books. They may decide to divide up the content to be covered among themselves or to work with different references on all the content. Part of the time they will be out of the classroom working in the school or public library. They will be expected to pool their information and organize a report to be presented to the class orally and in writing.

Another committee consisting largely of eye-minded students will gather information from films, film-strips, slides and pictures. Their final report may be to show and to discuss a particularly good film; or they may assemble, display, and interpret some of the most meaningful pictures they used. A third group can gather information from people by interviewing or, if the subject allowed, by taking an opinion poll of parents, teachers, peers, or individuals of importance in the community. They may also listen to relevant tapes and recordings. Their findings can be presented in statistical charts or they may prefer to recapture their experiences by role-playing some of them for the class.

A fourth subgroup may react to the problems in the unit by painting or creating a mural or using some other medium for creative expression. The art works or possible posters they create should be displayed, explained, discussed, and evaluated for the class.

Within the days or weeks devoted to a unit of learning, the teacher will find many opportunities to work with small groups and help the students to plan, to resolve work problems, and to understand the issues being studied. He will also need to meet with individuals on their special problems of adjustment to the group, of accepting responsibilities, of living up to commitments, or of interpersonal relations. The teacher will have to find time to work on a one-to-one basis with students who have not yet learned to read. The leaders of the several committees will also need opportunities to meet with the teacher to discuss their problems and to get whatever training they need in leadership arts and skills.

In the fully departmentalized senior high school there is also a place for small group work which will provide individualized instruction. Committees may be formed by the teacher, or students may volunteer to join one or another on the basis of their special needs and interests. For example, a few students may wish to embark on a special fact finding mission in the community. Bulletin board committees are always needed. Small groups may be particularly interested in collecting relevant pictures, art objects, or, in science, rocks, leaves, flowers, or insects.

Responsibility for keeping track of and informing the class about significant radio and TV programs can be delegated to a small committee. Current events provide many opportunities for small groups of specialists whose reading levels do not need to be high. A few students may wish to secure, write invitations, prepare questions for, introduce, and send thank-you letters to speakers and resource persons. Securing, operating, and returning audiovisual equipment can always become the responsibility of a special group of boys. A subcommittee might accept the job of keeping a class log or diary and of making sure that students returning after absence are reoriented. When special events such as preparing for an assembly program, a party, a dance, or a trip are contemplated, several small committees will be needed.

A human relations committee would be a most helpful device to use in welcoming and orienting new students, in helping isolates become part of the group, in resolving interpersonal and intergroup tensions, in interpreting students' needs and behavior to the teacher, and in maintaining the limits to behavior set up by the students and the teacher.

Grouping into so-called committees within the classroom is of no value unless the individual pupils in each group have meaningful work to do. It is not enough for one of a group of four or five to be doing something while the others stand around and look on. Neither is it a good idea for a group to break up a large problem or area of information into small rather insignificant questions to be doled out to the members of the group as their sole responsibility for the duration of the unit. A total problem must be the responsibility of the entire group—the differences being the kinds of resources to be used by individual pupils. Sometimes the form of classroom organization is used to cover the fact that nothing meaningful is taking place. The following descriptions of actual classrooms illustrate the point.

The eighth grade science class was divided into four groups. A visitor on entering the room thought "Fine! At last a teacher who isn't addicted to mass instruction." A closer look revealed that one group consisted of five girls who were huddled around one desk. On it a large sheet of paper was spread unevenly atop a pile of books. One girl was trying to copy on to that paper, from the textbook, a chart called "A Calendar for Bird Migrations." Four girls were looking on, doing nothing. In another part of the room a group of four boys were standing around another desk. One of them had a book in which he had turned to some small pictures of rocks. He held the book. Another boy had a small box in which there were a few stones. He picked up one at a time and held it against the picture in the book. The task given to this group was to classify the rocks. A third small group were around another desk. One pupil had a dictionary; another was writing words suggested by a third child which were looked up in the dictionary and dictated to her. Two others looked on. The teacher wandered from group to group, saying nothing.

Although Christmas was four weeks ahead, the sixth grade was using the English period to prepare for the holiday. The teacher had divided the class into groups each of which was responsible for something different. One group of four boys were crowded around one desk. They had a single copy of an old edition of one of the news sheets to which teachers often require children to subscribe. The "work" assigned to this group was to look through the paper to find ideas for a Christmas play. (The boys could not read the paper let alone write a play.) One boy was idly turning the pages; the others were doing nothing. At a table in the front of the room, four girls were "working" on a "mural." One had pasted a large sheet of paper over a chalkboard. One was cutting out stencilled stars. Two were watching with nothing to do—so was the teacher. In the middle of the room four boys were crowded around a desk. One of them had a dictionary in which he was looking up words. Their job was to think up and find out how to spell words about Christmas. Around a table were six girls who, as the consultant entered the room, burst into song; one girl had an old songbook in her hands. The group was supposed to find and learn new songs for the Christmas play.

This kind of make-believe distorts individualization of instruction as well as group-work. It disgusts pupils and destroys their trust in teachers and in the whole educational process.

LEARNING STYLES

Individuals differ with respect to what they require to initiate and to sustain the learning process. For example, reaction time may be fast or slow—one student can respond to a stimulus quickly, another needs a longer time before what he sees or hears seems to register. Their bodies may move quickly or at a leisurely pace. The slow reactors approach and get into a job more slowly than others. It takes them longer to gather their thoughts together. If the teacher fails to wait a little for them to answer questions, they give up trying. They must have more time to finish a task or a shorter task. In all probability they will not become rapid readers—this does not mean that they will not learn to read unless speed is demanded of them and they become tense and discouraged. They will be unable to keep up if the teacher requires them to do the same number of mental arithmetic problems at the same pace as their more rapidly reacting classmates. The teacher must look for quality rather than quantity of work accomplished when he evaluates their progress.

Children differ with respect to the amount of encouragement they need to attack a learning task, to persist when it becomes difficult, to continue when they become a little tired. If the teacher fails to recognize their need, these pupils stop working too soon and so fail to develop sufficient attention spans and qualities of persistence and diligence. The teacher who is sensitive to signs and signals meets the need for more encouragement with eye contacts, a pat on the back, a smile, a whispered word, and especially with praise for what the child has already done.

Children differ with respect to the amount, frequency, and kind of motivation for learning they require. Some have an inner drive for learning. They are interested in everything; they like school and books and teachers. They are eager to learn even without reference to the future. Other pupils must see a reason for every task with which they are confronted. Some boys must be convinced that what they are expected to learn has relevance for the job at which they hope to earn a living. Such a boy may say, "Why do I have to learn science? I'm going to be a truck driver."

All children, especially as they get older, are deeply concerned with their own development. There are some who, though they can see their physical growth, are not sure about what is happening to their minds. They need constant proof that they can learn. Success, getting things right, is the proof they must have. Praise and reward for learning, whether it comes slowly or rapidly, whether it is much or little at a time, are the best motivations. Some children require more frequent praise and reward than others. The teacher has to know who they are and receive with pleasure whatever they do well, get right, and create in writing, art, construction, or any other evidence they produce that they are learning.

Children differ in the amount of prodding they require. Some have been reared at home on the slogan, "Whatever is worth doing is worth doing well." Others have never been asked to show what they have done; they are not held accountable for their time; no one cares whether or not a job is finished. The teacher must recognize the effect of these varying past experiences on learning styles and without nagging or publicity make sure that those who need it get the supervision, the direction, the reminders they require to keep at a job, to do the best they can, and to be satisfied with no less. At the same time the teacher must know that the "best" will differ from one child to another and that the same degree of excellence cannot be an arbitrary standard for all. On the other hand, some children learn best when they are let alone. Constant supervision irks them.

Children differ with respect to the amount of concrete materials they must work with and the length of time they need before they can move to the abstract. For example, some can jump with ease from depending on the abacus and working with cuisenaire rods, to number symbols and from things to word symbols, while others must have more experience with concrete things and possibly must return to them again and again before concepts are completely understood, and symbols easily used. Children from impoverished backgrounds who have little experience in their first four or five years, may be quite unable to imagine and visualize things for which some words stand. Even pictures may not be enough for some. The learning centers proposed here are of great importance to those children. As they get older their teachers must provide experiences for them, must take them outside the classroom to experience at first hand the physical, social, political, and working world.

Children differ with respect to how much they rely on eyes or ears for learning. Some are said to be eye-minded while others are ear-minded. The former can learn more readily from word symbols that are printed or written, the latter do better when they hear the human voice either directly or through radio, TV, tapes, or recordings. Some eye-minded pupils can learn from pictures more easily than from word symbols. They may need to write down what they want to remember. Writing may not be a necessary prop for ear-minded children. The teacher must become aware of these differences in learning styles and provide for them in both teaching and home assignments.

INDEPENDENT LEARNING

Independent learning has long been the prerogative, if not the privilege, of academically able pupils who have been encouraged to undertake special projects for extra credit. The projects, not necessarily of great difficulty, are intended to carry the student into greater depth, to provide "enrichment" (although these are often the very children who have had much enrichment in their out of school lives), and to give plenty of homework. Usually the only in-school time allowed for them is that set aside for the class to hear what they have learned. These final reports too often consist of pages of information copied from reference books which the pupil reads to his bored and inattentive classmates.

Of course some independent learning projects are creative, but they are usually the ones connected with parents' interests and occupations. Very often parents assist their children with these projects especially if the products are to be exhibited in community-wide fairs where they compete for prizes. Consequently most of them are in one or another science field (medicine, biology, physics, chemistry, electronics, or space) or in the arts (painting, ceramics, or sculpture).

The concept of education as a process through which every individual must learn to learn means that learning has to be done by the individual for the purpose of his own development. The theorists say it is for self-realization or self-actualization. This means, then, that every child, no matter what his degree of brilliance, must become able to work at learning independently. If this is so, independent learning projects can no longer be thought of as special opportunities or privileges for academically able children to develop special skills which only they will need.

Independent learning activities for ordinary or slow learning pupils will differ in many respects from those undertaken by children who have larger capacities for work, broader interests, richer backgrounds, and probably more space and encouragement to work on them at home. These differences, however, should not make them less worthy. The suggestion here is that any question a child asks can become the initiative for an independent learning project for him. Instead of answering the question, the teacher can say, "Why not get to work finding the answer for yourself? Let us sit down together and make a plan, decide how you will work, where you will go and what you should do to find out what you want to know. You will make the plan; I will help you. When you are ready you can tell the class what you learned." Some children will need much help at first, others will soon catch on to the planning process and be eager to work by themselves. The extent of "research" required, the number of sources to be used, the depth of learning to be required all will have to be tailored to the learning style, the maturity and the levels of required skills the individual possesses.

Centers for direct sensory learning experiences will accustom children to use their senses to find out many things they want to know. They must also learn to learn from people, pictures, and tapes made for them by the teacher. Stories on tapes and discs can be used as sources of information about people, human relations, and behavior. Printed materials of all kinds must be available so that as soon as the individual child can do so, he will turn to the printed word.

It will not be possible for the teacher to set up standards by which to judge these projects. His greatest interest should be to gauge the individual's increasing ability to learn. Each project would have to be accepted on its own merits. Motivation should be to learn not to get marks or extra credit. Variations in how learnings are expressed should be encouraged and welcomed. For example, one child may just tell what he learned while another may put it into writing. Depending on the subject, a child may collect some pictures to show, while another may make his own illustrations. One child may make something relevant out of wood but another may do better with clay. A child may be able to express what he learned in physical movements to which another may be able to add music.

The kinds of things children want to know which teachers can use to initiate independent learning projects have been researched by a survey team—Ruth Byler, Gertrude Lewis, and Ruth Totman. Their findings are available in a report called "teach us what we want to know," published by the Mental Health Materials Center, 419 Park Ave. South, New York, N.Y. 10016. From grades 1 to 6, children want to find out about babies. In grades six through eight curiosity is centered on puberty, sex, and social problems. The latter recur in grades nine through twelve. Diseases are of concern to fourth, seventh, and tenth graders. Questions about alcohol, smoking, and drugs come up at the fifth, sixth, seventh and tenth grade levels. The drug epidemic in children from age ten up has now reached such proportions that it should become curriculum content of first priority whether or not pupils raise questions about it.

Independent learning projects for pupils of all levels of ability, that is, finding out for oneself from more than one source instead of getting answers to questions solely from the teacher or the textbook, can be concerned with matters of health; the structure of the human body (its functions and growth); differences in race and religion; first aid and safety; fears, emotions and mental health; human relations with friends and family; sex and reproduction in plants, animals and human beings; problems of living in the neighborhood, school and nation; poverty; discrimination and prejudice in the school and in the community; crime and violence; drug usage; civil rights (specific, not general); events of all kinds reported by the news media; and concrete objects of special interest such as wheels, cars, planes, tools, toys, and mechanical devices; and structures such as bridges, skyscrapers, and houses.

In "Education and Reality," a report on a study of development and curriculum, Frank Miceli says, "An overwhelming proportion of the questions asked (by adolescents) dealt with fear of social rejection, tenuousness of friendship, sexual exploration, breaking away from parental control, success in college or in a job, and fear of immaturity."

Meeting the Needs of High Ability Pupils
TO BECOME INDEPENDENT LEARNERS

Individualization does not mean that each child must be taught individually every day by the teacher, nor does it mean that every child must receive the same amount of the teacher's time each day. In fact to individualize that way may very well be the least effective way of meeting the needs of some children, especially those who have high academic or creative ability. These are the very ones who need and should want to work on their own without the constant supervision of the teacher, without the threat or reward of marks.

Children should be given opportunities to develop the skills of independent learning as early as possible. Even second graders can work by themselves. At all grade levels they need encouragement, guidance, follow-up, praise, and the rewards that come when they share their work and talents with their classmates.

The teacher's role in developing independent learners is similar at all age levels. Younger and less experienced pupils need more help, older ones want less "interference." In general, the teacher must help, but not dominate or dictate, in the choice of a subject on the basis of needs and interests; he must assist the student to make his plan, indicate where the sources of information can be found, and identify places and people who would be useful.

All the planning for a project need not be done at the outset, especially if the subject or project is complex. The first thing is to get going. After that the teacher must be sure that he includes in his daily plans time for the independent learners to consult with him or to show him their progress. Both individual conferences and small group meetings with these students will be needed from time to time. These can take place when the rest of the group are at work or when the learning centers are in use. Unless transportation problems forbid, meetings can also occur before or after the school day. The teacher must also set times for individual pupils to make progress and final reports to the class.

The quantity and quality of "research" to be expected should be appropriate to the individual student's physical and mental maturity as well as to the intrinsic values of the matter under study. Marks and grades or "extra-credit" for independent learnings will tend to obscure if not to prevent attainment of their objectives. If the goals set up are to learn to learn independently and to experience sharing self with others, the marks which children often regard as "pay" and toward which they direct their efforts, should be omitted altogether. Evaluation and praise should be expressed in words and appreciation in applause by both teacher and classmates. Written reports, maps, charts, posters, paintings, and all other illustrative materials included in the project should, of course, be placed on display where classmates and visitors have plenty of opportunity to examine and praise.

Excellent and realistic independent learning projects useful in upper elementary grades and secondary schools can be the outcome of discussion of events reported in the press, radio, and television. Students can be inspired to emulate their favorite commentators by becoming specialists or "watchers" of specific countries, people, or chains of events. For example, there should be some who are eager to be "China Watchers" or student demonstration watchers or specialists on the Middle East. Others may want to concentrate on civil rights or the President or Congress. There is no limit to the possibilities for special projects connected with current events. Moreover these independent studies would do much to vitalize a subject that in so many classes is unutterably dull.

A student who accepts responsibility for an independent learning project, when it is relevant to do so, should be encouraged to organize a small committee to assist him. It should include classmates of any ability level willing to work under his direction. They can, for example, help him gather pictures, headlines and printed materials for bulletin board displays or make posters, diaoramas, and other illustrative materials. Through such extension of his work, the high ability student learns also to organize, direct, and work with people different from himself. He gets training and experience in leadership.

In addition to gathering facts and organizing them into a meaningful report, the project leader should be responsible for notifying the class of relevant radio and TV broadcasts. The independent learner should be permitted to work outside the classroom and not be expected to do all his work at home. There are times when he should be in the library, in the science laboratory, in the office to interview a visitor, or elsewhere as his need dictates.

Teachers report that independent learning projects solve some behavior problems; that some nonreaders become good readers; that rejectees become accepted group members; that some apathetic pupils become eager and excited about learning.

TO BECOME LEADERS

High ability students should not spend all their time on independent projects for they need to learn and practice being leaders in a democratic society. One way to provide them with this kind of experience is to appoint them as assistant teachers. A pupil gets high praise and recognition when his teacher tells him he has learned well enough to teach others. This post carries prestige and status. The appointment is not only a reward, it is also a chance to consolidate learning—a person never knows anything so well as when he must teach it to another.

If the nation's brightest boys and girls are to become future leaders in education, politics, and civic and social affairs, they need, while in school, to experience the personal satisfaction and rewards that come from sharing with others, the joy of service that comes to dedicated teachers, administrators, doctors, and other professional "public servants." In a democratic society effective leadership requires positive attitudes toward human differences in race, color, creed, ethnic origins, social class, and mental ability. Experience with classmates in a helping relationship dispels the tendency of some bright pupils to look down on less well endowed peers.

TO SHARE THEIR TALENTS

Teachers ask if teacher assistants should always be the same students. No, they should not be and are unlikely to be if they are selected because they have what it takes to help others with specific learning tasks rather than because they are generally bright or "do the right thing" or have high IQ's. Pupils who should not be overlooked are those who have specialized abilities for which they should be recognized and rewarded. For example, a pupil whose reading level is below grade may be excellent in arithmetic and so should become a teacher assistant in that subject. A very good artist may be the one to head up a group working on a mural for the classroom or to act as a teacher assistant when the class is doing any kind of art work. Bilingual pupils could assist their classmates in Spanish, for example, but not in English. High ability in social studies may not be coupled with high ability in science. Moreover there is considerable evidence that a pupil need not necessarily have achieved excellence in reading to be able to assist a classmate who reads less well than he does and that in so doing the reading skills of both improve.

Using students to help others is clearly a method of individualizing instruction. Through one-to-one tutoring relationships in heterogeneous groups, some of the learning needs of bright, average, and slow pupils can be met.

8 MARKS AND REPORT CARDS

"... The most adequate model of proper education in all subjects is the classroom where each one's talents are relevant; where every child's products are valued equally insofar as they emanate from equally worthy children; where children are not pitched competitively against each other, not denigrated or honored for "higher achievements"; where each proceeds in accordance with his own unique tempo of development; and where at any given moment the child moves on to tasks for which he is ready, as defined by his own prior work and achievements."

Melvin Tumin
"Report on the Arts and the Poor"
HEW, Office of Education, 1968

Marks and Report Cards

The December, 1970 issue of *Today's Education—NEA Journal* contained a report of a nationwide survey of what schools are doing about report cards. It indicates that "83 percent of secondary teachers and 71 percent of elementary teachers are using report cards with classified scales of letters. However, some 60 percent of the elementary teachers supplement the card with conferences with parents, while only 20 percent of the secondary teachers engage in scheduled conferences with parents. Almost 25 percent of the elementary teachers reported that they provide parents with a written description of the pupil's performance, as compared with 10 percent of the secondary teachers. Report cards with pass or fail designations are used by 8 percent of the elementary teachers and 2.6 percent of the secondary teachers."

The study noted that the *report card* is gradually being supplanted by *progress report* and that schools are revising these instruments to provide parents with more detailed information in terms of the development of pupil skills. Nevertheless, many pupil progress reports place their emphasis almost entirely on the subjects in the curriculum rather than on the learner while many teachers and administrators reveal a greater concern about *how* to report than *what* to report.

The requirement that pupils get marks for everything they

do, the attempt at regular intervals to summarize dozens of discrete evaluations into single symbols to put on report cards for parents, and the promotion of pupils from one grade to the next on the basis of marks constitute the greatest barriers to development and use of methods of individualizing instruction. Formalized and uniform marking systems defeat teachers' efforts to provide success experiences for slow learners and for children who are handicapped by having uneducated parents and who live in poverty-stricken environments. Moreover, they support the "pass-fail" concept which is unrelated to both the principle of individual growth and development and the school's basic responsibility for developing each child's unknown potentialities to the fullest extent.

Strange situations and practices develop when teachers try to meet individual needs. For example, they group "according to ability," use outmoded grading systems often handed down by state departments of education, "maintain standards" which require the use of arbitrary dividing lines between "pass" and "fail," promote in terms of chronological age for social adjustment purposes, compare children who are not comparable, and satisfy parents who want high marks for their own children regardless of what these children have learned or how much they have grown.

In some school systems where grouping by ability (really tracking) is used, pupils on the second level cannot get marks above B (if the scale is A, B, C, D, E, or F), and those in the lowest groups cannot be graded more than C no matter how well they do their classroom work. This practice, which deprives children of marks commensurate with the quality of the work they produce, negates the claim that marks are used as incentives to effort. Why should a pupil strive to do well when he knows his success will go unrewarded?

There are other systems in which teachers are not restricted in the marks they may give but are required to indicate on reports to parents the grade level of the work the child is doing if it is below the grade in which he is placed. However, the teacher does not usually indicate on the reports that pupils are working above grade level. Thus, for example, a sixth grade child in a low group or in a mixed group may receive A for arithmetic on his report card but somewhere on it the parent finds that he is doing only fourth grade work. Some parents are so eager to have their children rated A that they ask to have them placed in lower level classes "so they can get high marks without having to work so hard."

Among the unfortunate outcomes of marking schemes currently required by some state departments of education are the labels that get attached to pupils. For example, in at least one state a child is called "superior" if he is marked from 100 to 95, but if the mark is only one point lower, 94, he is called "above average." This may not seem to be so bad, but at the lower end of the scale it becomes more serious. There a child marked 70 is called average but for one point less he may be labeled for all time to come in school "below average." It is ridiculous to suppose that teachers can measure children's accomplishments, their growth and development, let alone their potentials, so precisely. It is unthinkable that on decisions based on such intangible evidence some children are led to believe they are inferior.

Teachers are confused about marks. They do not see how they can fairly mark pupils who, though they sit in the same classroom, differ from each other by as many as two, three, or even four grades in their levels of achievements. Some resist the idea that a child should be given credit for whatever he does right. If a given task is below the grade level, teachers do not believe it should get a top mark even though it may be done perfectly. They cannot see how they can give marks for learning to learn when they know that pupils learn in different ways at different rates and require different lengths of time to do the same amount of work. They are anxious to do away with marks but find many others to blame for keeping them: the "system," the principal, the administration, the state department and, most of all, the parents and the colleges.

It is high time for all connected with education to face the absurdity of outmoded marking and reporting practices, the impossibility of combining and averaging dozens of discrete items into one letter or number symbol, and the conscious or unconscious values and attitudes that influence teachers' decisions when they make out report cards.

Elementary schools generally use three-point scales: S (Satisfactory), U (Unsatisfactory), N (Needs improvement); sometimes O (Outstanding) is added. To whom the child is satisfactory, what makes him outstanding, and in what respect he needs to improve are often left to the imagination. Some schools have dispensed with these symbols and use only "pass" and "fail." The dangers surrounding this practice have already been discussed. Some children begin to learn to fail in kindergarten and never get over the habit.

Some secondary schools are using pass-fail marking schemes, but most of them use five-point scales which may be A, B, C, D, F or E, G, F, P, VP or 1, 2, 3, 4, 5 or 5, 4, 3, 2, 1. Both the three- and the five-point scales were designed to eliminate small gradations but teachers defeat that purpose by qualifying the symbols with plus or minus or subnumerals and by using additional symbols such as zero (0) and check (v). The meanings of all these differentiations are obscure, and the factors the teachers use to determine which to use with a given child differ from teacher to teacher and time to time.

It is necessary to examine the gradations and raise some questions about them. Does S+ mean more than satisfactory? Can that be? If it is, then why not outstanding? Is it possible to be just under outstanding and so get O−? If U+ is not unsatisfactory why not call it S? How can anyone believe that these are real distinctions based upon factual evidence upon which all teachers could agree? Why do parents and teachers regard these symbols as evidence of "standards"? If individuals do in fact differ widely in rates and levels of development, in nutrition, metabolism and general health, in the amount and quality of sleep they get, in causes and levels of anxiety, in learning styles, in environmental advantages, and in the amount of early childhood training they can possibly get in preparation for the middle class school, then how is it possible to judge their progress by any arbitrary set of "standards"? There are other related questions that remain unanswered and that plague parents and teachers: would it be better for a child to have a teacher who is lenient or one who is strict in marking; does one child have an advantage over another because he happens to be in a different room?

When a plus or a minus or a numeral modifies the values of the letter symbols, the five-point scale becomes a twenty-point scale, and the distinctions become more petty and more subject to the moods and whims and attitudes of the individual teacher.

Whether a given pupil receives B++, B+, B, B−, B−− or A$_1$, A$_2$, A$_3$, A$_4$, A$_5$ or C+, C− or C or even F or F− (whatever that could mean) may depend less on what he knows or has learned than on whether his work was done on time or whether his paper was clean and well-arranged or who his father is. Some teachers say they really are using percentages (A means anything from 100 to 90 and so on), but that does not really make them any more valid. There are still such questions as: does F+ indicate any more than failure; are there superlatives beyond A or E or O all of which are supposed to be the top marks; can someone do better than best; if there are such things as "standards" which teachers say they "must keep up," under what conditions do passing marks have to be 70 and under which can they be 68 or 65 or even 60; what is an "effort grade"; is "effort" the reason for adding a plus or a minus; what are the other reasons; how much is a plus worth?

Occasionally teachers say somewhat strange things about their marking practices. A high school teacher said, "I just love that little old boy, and I failed him. He took three courses with me and I failed him every time. But I just love that little old boy!" Most teachers talk about the marks they *give* pupils.

The whole pass-fail syndrome should be discarded because it has little if any relationship to individual growth and development patterns and because teachers do not agree with respect to the place where the dividing line should be drawn. Should a child pass if he spells 7 out of 10 words right most days? Does it make a difference which words he did not learn the night before or why he learned so little or so much? Should the words misspelled be the same for all children? Should a child pass arithmetic if he gets 7, or can it be 6, of 10 answers right? Does it matter whether the process is right or wrong as long as the answer is right? Which mark should be reduced if a child does not bring in his homework 4 days out of 5? Does the teacher know or care whether Mom or Dad or the whiz kid in the class does the assignment for the child? Would it matter that on the days homework was missing so was the child or that he was away because he was sick or truant or there was death in the family?

Teachers say, "Each child, each case must be decided on its

own merits." Good enough, but what constitutes "merit"? What factors influence decisions? Teachers are human. They have their own hang-ups, preferences, biases, prejudices, and fears. Is a teacher's judgment affected by the status of a child's father or by the mother's election to the presidency of the PTA? Or, does it make a difference if the parents never come or, in the teacher's judgment, "don't care"? Will decisions about the marks to be put on report cards depend upon whether it is the first or the middle or the final report for the year?

Again with respect to "standards." Are they always the same or is there a double standard applied to pupils of different races? Are standards related to cleanliness, to illegitimacy and to poverty by teachers who perceive some children as likely to "succeed in life," and others as "bound to fail"? If, in truth, the marks that appear on report cards are matters of judgment rather that numerical facts, would it not be better for teachers to say so to themselves, to the pupils, and to the parents? A teacher could say without hesitation and without feelings of guilt, "These marks represent my opinions, my best judgments, I did not and cannot calculate them mathematically." This, of course, would make the report card a personal matter between a child and his teacher. It could be as individualized as instruction must be. It could be determined on evidences of growth, development, and learning which are individual matters. There would be no necessity for one child or his parents to compare his card with that belonging to another and quite different child who just happens to be in the same classroom. All the energy that now goes into a relentless struggle for marks could be turned to learning for the sake of knowing and becoming the best that one can become.

A teacher's opinions, like everyone's, are heavily influenced by his value systems and attitudes. These often cause him to prejudge a child, especially a child who differs from himself. That, in turn, often determines what he expects the particular child to do, to achieve, to produce. Research studies have revealed that students at all age levels behave and learn pretty much as they are expected to do. Evidence is growing that the teacher's expectations about a pupil or a group not only affect his feelings about teaching them but also affect how and what he prepares for them to do. His expectations determine the quantity and quality of his instructional plans and procedures and, therefore, of the child's performance.

What then is to be done about marks and reports? Progress in learning and skill development must be indicated to both parent and pupil. Since it is not really possible to add and divide and thus come up with an average at the end of every six or nine or twenty weeks, why not use words instead of symbols to evaluate each task a child undertakes? If, when so doing, the emphasis is placed on what is *right* (a basic principle in learning), then, even though the number of words or examples a pupil has right may not be the same as another's, everyone who has anything right experiences success.

The necessity for giving every child a successful learning experience of some kind every day does not mean that the teacher must read and correct all the problems or all the spelling words on every paper every day or the entire composition or theme or report handed in. Instead, it is enough if he scans each paper, finds some things on it that are right, circles or checks and praises those, and tells the pupil to find others that are right, how to get help if he needs it to make more right, and then to bring it back. The teacher's constant admonition should be, "Show me your best work; I want to see it when you have everything right." Instead of saying, "That's wrong," would it be better to say, "Go back and look again."

Miss Barnes tried to do just that when she saw two words correctly spelled by a child who rarely had any right. She drew circles around them and at the top of the paper wrote 100. But, inasmuch as 100 is merely a symbol that means something is entirely right, she might better have placed it beside each correct word and have written at the top, "2 right! I'm delighted!" When Miss Barnes gave the paper back to Johnny, all he saw was the 100. His eyes popped open and he sat down so hard he fell off his chair. Miss Barnes helped him up saying, "Johnny, what's the matter?" The child replied, "Never in my whole life did I get 100 before!" Miss Barnes said, "Well you did today, and I know you will tomorrow too." The next day Johnny had all his words right.

Success in school means getting something right. Success motivates; it frees energy for learning; it increases effort. Failure kills motivation and creates anxiety, feelings of inadequacy and hope-lessness which inhibit learning. The teacher's expectation that Johnny would be successful the next day helped him to believe in his own ability to learn as well as in her interest in him and her desire that he should learn.

Learning logs described in connection with the use of learning centers, become vivid and vital records of success. They should be much more meaningful to parents than symbols on report cards. Parents may need to be taught the difference and helped to understand why old forms of marking and reporting must be abandoned.

Teachers at all levels find it possible to write one or two 3x5 cards about one or two pupils each day for them to take home to parents. These are best when written at the time the teacher observes a step forward or is especially pleased with a task well done. A pupil who has experienced success and has a card from the teacher to tell his parents about it goes home feeling a little better about himself and a little happier about being alive. There is no more effective public relations agent than such a child.

Secondary school teachers are terribly overburdened with paper marking. What they need to realize is that very often a student is overwhelmed by all the red marks they have so laboriously put on the paper. So, in order to cut their labor and give the student something he can handle, instead of marking an entire paper, they would do better to mark only a first or last or middle paragraph or sentence or problem and to leave the rest for the student to check, proofread, and edit. In some kinds of writings and reports, no attention need be given to correction of format or grammar or spelling, but rather at-tention should be given to discover whatever in the paper is true or beautiful or original—elements which should be recognized and praised rather than marked. There are times when one or two beautiful sentences are worth more than a whole page full of claptrap.

At all grade levels, pupils need the experience of checking the accuracy of their own work by going back to sources—the dic-tionary for spelling, tables and slide rules for computations, text and reference books for facts. Pupils can also help each other to look for and correct errors. The answers on tests, especially objective ones, ought to be checked at once, if at all possible, by the pupils themselves or by each other. A valid principle holds that immediate reinforcement promotes learning. Moreover, at the moment that he finishes taking a test, a pupil is eager to learn the correct answers. The object of any test should be for the pupil to find out what he knows as well as what he still needs to learn.

Many teachers believe that children must experience failure in school so they will not overestimate their abilities and will not be knocked down when they "fail in life." Such spurious reasoning is often used by secondary school teachers to justify assigning some students work which the teacher knows the student cannot do. For example, it is common practice to use a single text and to require all pupils to learn what is in it, even those who cannot read it. Too many teachers are sure that they know what potentialities each student has and are very anxious to make sure that students find out in their classrooms their "true limitations." There are no valid instruments for determining potentials. Fortunately many predictions of future failure have been quite wrong. Many of the qualities teachers look for and reward in school, as well as those that can be measured to some degree by available tests, are not necessarily those needed for success on the job in the working world or for effective living in our society. For example, many teachers do not enjoy or recognize creativity.

Evidence is increasing that failing in school does in fact make people inadequate for living and working successfully. Teachers are therefore obliged to help pupils to avoid failure which kills effort, creates a negative self-image, increases anxiety and may lead to physical, emotional or mental illness (even suicide), all of which block learning.

The injunction to eliminate failure is not to be taken as a directive to misrepresent the value of a piece of work. In fact teachers do that now with what is called "marks for effort." If a job is not well done but is accepted as satisfactory by the teacher who returns it saying sarcastically, "That's pretty good for you" or "I know you tried," the pupil is likely to react with disgust and distrust and to believe that his teacher does not really care whether or not he learns. Teachers are often heard to say, "He made a zero but I gave him a pass" (whatever that may mean).

A poor piece of work can be called poor without labeling it, and the person who did it, a *failure*. The pupil needs to know, however, what makes his work unacceptable. The teacher's responsibility is to help him to do a better job. If for some reason, which the teacher must determine, the task is beyond the pupil's capability, an easier one must be provided.

Every child has the right to make mistakes and even to forget. So has the teacher. Mistakes, however, should not be thought of as failures but rather as learning experiences and should be so used by both the teacher and the pupil.

Paper marking, like writing report cards, involves personal opinions and judgments which are affected by emotions, fatigue, and even the time of day or night or day of the week on which the task is being done. Conscious and subconscious prejudices affect decisions. They may be merely dislike or distaste or strong aversion or hatred for individual pupils especially for those who differ in race or religion or social class. They may reflect racism or anti-Semitism or anti-Catholicism. Some teachers are repelled by children who are too fat or too scrawny or too dirty—a quality some equate with immorality. One lad, son of a college professor, turned in a special paper on which he and his dad had worked hard and considered very good. When it was returned it was marked the same old C. At the father's suggestion, the boy questioned the teacher about his mark. Her answer was, "You may as well know it now. I just don't like you, and you will never get any other mark from me."

Social class affects teachers' attitudes and behavior. A research study proved that children of white-collar families got more smiles, more pats on the back, more encouragement, more time to answer questions than did children of blue-collar families.[1]

---

[1] Mildred B. Smith, unpublished doctoral thesis. "Interpersonal Influence on the Occupational and Educational Aspirations and Expectations of Sixth Grade Students" (unpublished Ph.D. dissertation, Michigan State University, 1961).

9 COMPETITION

"Within the competition of people with each other for scarce rewards, there is no room for compassion. Let them compete instead in assisting each other, in furthering the excitement and beauty of their experience, in helping each other to grow and develop. Let the child in all the years of growing up, live compassionately and with enlightenment, and let the quest for these qualities be given the priority to which human dignity is entitled."

Herbert A Thelen
"Comments on What it Means to Become Humane," Chapter 6
Association for Supervision and Curriculum Development,
To Nurture Humaneness, Yearbook 1970

Competition

Teachers fear that individualization of instruction means doing without competition in learning. They are disturbed not only because they believe that competition is the best way to get pupils to work hard but also because they are convinced that our society is "run by competition." They say they cannot prepare pupils to *make a living* unless they teach them how to compete. They seem to ignore their equal responsibility for preparing pupils to *make a life*.

Effective personal living in a democratic society requires cooperation. Moreover, very few, if any, occupations involving two or more people can be carried on successfully without good human relations which depend upon skill in cooperation. In addition, stable and happy family life, essential for the physical and mental health of children, is impossible when parents and siblings compete rather than cooperate with each other.

Both competition and cooperation are democratic processes which require values, understandings, insights, and skills which the school does have responsibility to transmit to each succeeding generation. Therefore activities and experiences which afford practice of both processes belong in the curriculum. The question is to what extent an individual child's learning is helped or inhibited by competition in the classroom.

According to the dictionary the concept of competition includes struggle between or among people who are more or less *evenly matched*. It also implies the possibility of unfriendliness and even hostility. Every classroom group is made up of pupils who differ from each other to such an extent they cannot possibly be considered evenly matched. Moreover, any activity that promotes unfriendliness and hostility is antithetical to development of good human relations and groupness essential for the kind of classroom climate that contributes to constructive behavior and accomplishment on the part of all members of the class.

In classrooms dominated by competition there develops a general atmosphere of anxiety and some apathy. The pupil who despairs of winning retreats from the struggle. To protect himself he may decide that he doesn't care or doesn't want to win. In this way he makes school unimportant so that his failure may become unimportant.

Competition in the classroom developes a general lack of concern about what happens to anyone other than oneself. It becomes a matter of "me first and the devil take the hindmost!" In newly desegregated classrooms, white pupils have even been known to threaten and abuse their black classmates who do too well. Furthermore, studies have shown that black students at all levels, in competition with whites, are likely to do less than their best for fear of increasing the hostility directed against them.

When the classroom goal is status, competition for it is likely to be far too stiff for pupils disadvantaged by reason of lower social class values and lack of motivation in the home and neighborhood. When a student finds himself defeated by such odds, he may drop out of the race altogether and seek status in his peer group outside of school. There, winning is likely to depend upon the use of fists rather than mind, on being able to get money somehow, on being able "to make it" with the opposite sex.

Individualization of instruction precludes the idea that the classroom is the scene and setting for a race for the purpose of selecting a winner. Teachers, parents and pupils have to accept the principle that *each individual is the winner in his own right when he learns*. The school's aim is to fulfill its primary responsibility of developing the unknown potentialities of each and every child so that someday he may become what he can become. This requires cooperative effort, not competition, on the part of all concerned.

Some teachers believe that individualized assignments, the use of materials that vary in difficulty, and evaluations based upon the quality of performance of tasks suited to varying levels of ability and achievement will make bright pupils resentful and will reduce their motivation and efforts. According to those teachers high ability pupils, deprived of the stimulus of competition in which they are bound to be the winners, will say, "Why do hard work when others get good marks and praise for doing easy work?" Indeed, that may occur but when it does it raises the questions: "Are these our future leaders, already unconcerned about what happens to others? Are they surrendering their capacities for enjoyment learning in order to get good marks?" If that does happen, teachers would do well to reexamine their own feelings and behavior towards pupils of different ability levels. Children both sense and copy their teachers' attitudes and actions. In such situations, the chances are that the teacher is overemphasizing competition, making unfair comparisons, pitting pupils against each other, and looking on those who do well as "the winners." It may even be that everyone has come to think of marks as "pay" for work done for the teacher.

Individualization requires that bright pupils be confronted with materials and tasks commensurate with their abilities and challenged to do their best work. They, like others, need the reinforcement that comes from praise and recognition. One of the best rewards for these boys and girls is appointment to the position of teacher assistant. This gives them the chance to help less gifted peers rather than to look down upon them. Moreover, when the teacher emphasizes equality of opportunity and every individual's responsibility for learning, unequal rivalries for marks are likely to disappear.

Personal evaluation is essential for a pupil to do his best work. That calls for something more from the teacher than his constantly repeated and practically meaningless "all right" or "OK." Recitations and contributions to discussion should bring such acknowledgements as "Good," "Fine," "Excellent," "I like that," "You have helped us," "I understand," "I get your point." These and many others are meaningful words and phrases that evaluate and encourage participation. The group, too, should be permitted to praise and applaud work that is well done, regardless of the level involved.

Excessive or even moderate use of competition in the classroom may affect the group's morale, if in such games as spelling bees and question and answer contests, teams selected at random or by sex are pitted against each other, and individuals who do not know the answers are taunted or even punished by members of their own teams. Danger also exists when popular or very able team leaders appointed by the teacher choose their own teams. Those children who wait and wait, are the last to be chosen, and may then hear groans from team mates, have very bitter experiences.

When morale is high, a class group is likely to be responsive nondistractible, good humored, and productive. Low morale contributes to apathy, sullenness, inability to understand instructions, doggedness, interpersonal aggressions, and expressions of inadequacy. Where competition as the way of life and getting higher marks than classmates becomes the objective, stress and tension reduce morale. Those who "go down," and those who cannot possibly win often become bored, feel unrewarded, unappreciated, and that they have no place in the classroom. In response the teacher does more and more, often all, the talking, acting and thinking.

Gardiner Murphy, writing in "Human Potential," says, "Competition . . . frustrates and benumbs most of those who fail, and for those who succeed, it can at best, give only the ever iterated satisfaction of winning again. This may destroy the ability to risk failures for the sake of attempting new and more interesting goals. In the direction of competition . . . lies a convenient way of maintaining a status minded society . . . (but not) the release of human potential."

10 WHAT CHILDREN ABSORB ABOUT LEARNING

"A classroom is a kind of weather system. Just as we take on the mood of the day, being drawn toward cheerfulness or gloom according to whether the day is sunny or overcast, so students tend to internalize the psychic climate of their schools. The chief controls in this climate are its teachers."

Huston Smith, "Condemned to Meaning"
John Dewey Society Lecture, N.Y.: Harper and Row, 1965

Children Absorb Negative Ideas About Learning

Teachers who see classrooms as places in which the most important activity is teaching and who believe that what they *teach* matters more than what each child learns are often unaware of the ideas their pupils unconsciously absorb about learning. These ideas come from what the teachers do and say, do not do and do not say, and from the teachers' general attitudes toward the subject matter.

For example, children get the idea that *learning is a privilege* to be granted or withheld with or without reason or explanation. In a second grade room, the children were in a huddle around the table at which the teacher, using concrete materials, was telling and showing how to do subtraction. When she believed she had done enough, she said, *"Now I'll let you do some examples at your desks."* Some children clapped their hands; others said, "Oh, goody"; they all scampered to their places. Sometimes the idea is conveyed more directly. A high school teacher said to his class when they were resisting his instruction, *"Education is a privilege for which you should be grateful."*

In very many classrooms, pupils absorb the idea that *learning is something you do for the teacher.* In the first grade room, eight children were seated around the teacher for their reading lesson.

Miss Thompson made sure to impress upon them that they were working for her rather than for themselves or each other. As she called on each child in turn, she said, "John, read the next paragraph *to me*"; "Mary, *show me* where to find the answer to that question"; "Tommy, break down that word *for me*"; "Sue, *tell me* what that sentence means."

In the fourth grade room, when the class was ready to review the arithmetic homework, Mrs. Wright said, "John, put the first example on the board *for me*"; "Jane, while Harry is doing the second one *for me,* will you distribute the science books *for me.*"

A third idea that most students, at all grade levels, absorb about learning is that the *teacher is the fountainhead* of learning; therefore he is the only one to whom they must listen. The teacher conveys this thought most effectively by repeating every answer every child gives. By so doing, he gives pupils the idea that nothing they say is sufficiently important or good enough for anyone else to listen to. So, finding it unnecessary to listen to classmates' answers in a recitation period, they remain uninvolved until specific questions are directed to them and again lose interest once they have answered.

Children soon absorb the idea that they should expect school to be dull, that *there is no fun about learning.* Many secondary school teachers present new material with so little enthusiasm that they convey the idea that they are not excited about the subject and really do not care whether or not the students learn it. The excitement which might be generated in interpersonal student reaction is inhibited when they are not allowed to talk to each other. After a lecture the students are not given a chance to raise questions; they are directed to read the book and find the answers to the questions at the end of the chapter. There can be little pleasure or excitement or challenge in reading the textbook, especially for those who cannot read.

When the lectures and the books deal with what is distant, often remote, in time and space, when the content has little or no relation to the realities of their lives in the here and now, many teenagers reject the subject, the teacher, the school, and eventually education. Too many classrooms are dull and full of hostility. The only time students laugh is when they make fun of their classmates or the teacher. Both children and teen-agers describe their feelings about school by saying, "It stinks"; "It's boring"; "I hate it"; "I wish I could leave"; "I don't learn anything"; "It's no fun."

For many years teachers have been urged to use audio-visual aids, and some do use films, filmstrips, slides, overhead projectors and transparencies, radio and television. However, in school, pupils are convinced that *the best, if not the only, way to learn is to read and memorize the book.* "Well," they say, "that's the only way you can get a good mark, so why fight it?" The children, at all levels absorb this idea because recitation and test questions are taken from the chapters in the book that have been assigned for home study. Too often the only questions discussed in class are those at the end of those chapters. In some instances the only acceptable answer is the one which uses the words used in the book. Verification of facts by consulting other books or other sources for differences of opinions is not encouraged much less required. Students are given little if any opportunity to express their own ideas and opinions especially if they differ from the textbook author or the teacher.

Especially in elementary school, children absorb the thought that *learning is not sufficiently important to take up all the time.* So much time is wasted and the pace is so slow. Many times during the day children wait with nothing to do while the teacher, committed to mass instruction, waits for the slow-pokes to put pencils down or clear their desks or get out their books or sit down or get up or get quiet. So often learning tasks are too little, too trivial, too boring for many children. One day a six year old showed his daddy a large paper on which he had written I's until the paper was covered with them. "Daddy," he asked, "why do I have to do all this? The teacher knows I can make an I." In a second grade class, when children returned from their reading circle, their only job was to copy the single sentence the teacher had written on the board. In many classrooms pupils not engaged in the reading group spend their time doing "busy-work," which consists solely of coloring stencils or of copying from the board or the workbook, letters and words which they cannot name or read.

Even more time is wasted in elementary schools that are departmentalized or in which children are regrouped for reading and arithmetic. When the time comes to change classes, it is time to line up—line up to leave the room, then line up in the corridor to wait until the next teacher has her children lined up to leave her room. Soon it is time for recess or, as it is now called, "for a break." That again means line up to leave the room; line up in the yard to come back into the building; line up outside the classroom door until the teacher is ready to let them in. Then lunch time comes so, line up to leave the room and to walk down the hall; line up outside the lunchroom door; line up to get the tray; line up to leave after eating; line up to get back into the room when the teacher gets there to open the door. At last the day is over, so it is time to get ready to go home which may mean waiting in line as much as ten minutes for the bell to ring. Then, once more it is line up to leave the room on the way to freedom from lines.

Far too many children absorb the idea that *it is not necessary to exert effort to learn quickly* for if they do so they will just have to wait until the others catch up. Unless learning tasks are assigned on the basis of maturity, reading levels and learning rates and styles, children who react quickly, get to work fast, or have an inner drive to learn are just out of luck. They are likely to get into mischief or become bored or escape into dreaming if they are forced into idleness by a teacher who uses only mass instruction aimed at the "average" child and then waits for the slowest to do what he may be quite unable to do.

So much emphasis is placed on marks and report cards that children are bound to absorb the idea that *the reason for learning is to get good marks.* Once that objective is achieved, it is no longer necessary to remember the subject matter. This belief is strengthened by the widespread practice of conducting recitations in turn. A pupil needs to pay attention only until the teacher reaches him. Then he can turn his attention to other things. He needs to know only the answer to the question directed to him.

The stress and strain produced by competition for marks, especially at the secondary school level, as well as the fears generated by parents' negative reactions to lower marks often interfere with learning. Sometimes anxiety over marks results in nervous and even mental breakdown. This becomes particularly severe after high school when a "straight A" student finds in college that he has not *learned to learn.* It is also responsible for the practice of cheating in both high school and college by competent students.

11 HOW DO YOU TURN THEM ON?

"To meet the needs of students it will be necessary to involve them deeply. This will not be easy, for traditional practices have done their work well—our students are thoroughly brainwashed into the belief that learning is a passive process in which you are not learning anything unless someone is telling you something and that independent action gets you nowhere."

Arthur W. Combs
"An Educational Imperative: The Human Dimension," Chapter 17
Association for Supervision and Curriculum Development,
To Nurture Humaneness, Yearbook 1970

How Do You Turn Them On?

What many teachers want to know is how do you turn children on—how do you get them to participate; how do you keep them involved? That is what this book is about. The answers that we know will work (we do not have all the answers by any means) are so important they are worth restating with some additional stories to illustrate what goes on in actual classrooms.

If you who are, or will be, teachers want to turn your pupils on you must do the following:

Relate to them. First of all, *see* them—keep them with you through frequent eye contact. Turn your head while you talk to them instead of looking only at those who sit directly in front of you. Move around the room as you teach and as the pupils work. Go quickly to the child whose face, posture, or activity shows he is slipping away. Put your hand on his arm, stoop quickly to whisper a word of warning in his ear. Do not talk to the class from the rear of the room and ask the pupils to talk to you without facing you. As often as possible arrange the furniture so that the students can face each other as they interact, instead of having to look only at the backs of each other's heads. Look at what pupils are writing during the time they spend on "busy work"; help every child who needs it.

Children want the teacher to *see* them personally. A junior high school teacher was working at her desk before the day began. Pupils were coming in as they arrived at the building. Each one greeted her, "Good morning Mrs. Morgan," and she returned their greetings, "Good morning." One child repeated her greeting, "Good morning, Mrs. Morgan." The teacher, knowing the voice, looked up at the child, "I did say good morning to you, Sally." "Yes, you did, Mrs. Morgan," said Sally, "but I wanted you to see that it was *me* who said good morning to you."

Nothing is more devastating for a child than not being seen by a teacher. Mr. Scott was conducting a discussion. He asked a question and waited for one or more pupils to raise their hands to answer it. The first hand to go up belonged to a black boy seated in the third seat on the second row. Gradually other hands were raised and finally the teacher began to call on the children. He began with the last row and gradually moved to the first but skipped over the second. Then the lad whose hand had been up first lowered his arm. The period ended and he never did get a chance to make his contribution to the discussion. When a visiting consultant asked the teacher why that particular pupil, whom she described, was overlooked, the teacher could not recall that there was such a boy seated in that place, let alone that his was the first hand raised.

Make sure that each pupil succeeds. Every child should be able to go home at night feeling a little better about himself and a little happier about being alive. He will do so on the days he gets something right. Let that something be worthy of his effort and his ability—not just play.

A black college student told with bitterness, the following story of an experience she "could never forget." She said, "Mathematics has always been my best subject. I love it. One day in Geometry, the teacher put a problem on the board and said, 'It's a difficult problem. I don't expect many of you can do it.' I could do it, so I raised my hand. The teacher glanced at me, then turned away, and waited until a white boy raised his hand, and she asked him to put it on the board. Turning to me with what was intended to be a smile, she said, 'I'll give *you* an easier one to do later on.' "

Every pupil, no matter who he is and how he differs, needs to be built up, not broken down. Each one needs to see himself as beautiful, worthy and trustworthy; to experience equality of status in the mixed peer group; to find himself growing in his ability to cope with himself, with others, and with his world.

In an article, "What 70 SEEK Kids Taught Their Counselor,"[1] Linda Weingarten describes students fresh out of high school. She saw ". . . their bitterness, despair, self defeating behavior, frightening ignorance of the way society works," their inability to communicate. She raised questions: "What was the name of their disturbance—schizophrenia, paranoia, psychic trauma, character disorder?" She had an answer, *The disease was failure*—the cure for their economic problems, their wretched self evaluation which made them ignore opportunities, *was success*."

Teach every child how to learn. To do this requires that you know and pay attention to differences in levels of development and learning styles. It means you must rely much less on mass instruction. You will have to organize small groups in your classes, related to the learning tasks to be done and in terms of pupils' abilities. One-to-one help may be needed for able as well as reluctant learners when no other grouping will suffice. Some individuals need your personal help to learn to read, others need to be challenged to do work beyond the class level.

Create groupness. It is true that the individual's uniqueness needs to be recognized and cultivated, but in our society, in order to live effectively, individuals must also learn how to act effectively in various kinds of groups. People who differ move closer together, begin to see each other as important, good, and worth knowing when they discover that they have common problems, set up common goals, and decide how they will work together to reach their goals. Interest, hopefully excitement, in being a member of a classroom group creates loyalty to it, commitment to its purposes and willing participation in its activities. The methods and processes used to create groupness are those identified with democracy: planning, decision making, sharing labor, reporting progress and evaluating self, others, leaders, process, and product.

Let the students be with each other. As children grow older the peer group becomes increasingly important to them. The greatest punishment for the normal teen-ager, for example, is to be re-

1 N.Y. Times Magazine, Nov. 16, 1969—SEEK—Search for Education, Elevation and Knowledge.

moved from the group. When suspended from school, many a boy hangs around the school yard. Much disciplinary trouble can be avoided if this need is recognized and time is allotted for students to talk to each other.

Sometimes association should be free, without teacher supervision and without specific instructional purpose. Five or ten minutes to stretch, walk around the room, talk to friends, and possibly have a snack can be set by the teacher as a regular part of the day or the period, or it can be determined by signs of restlessness, fatigue, or boredom.

In addition to subgroup activities in units of learning, conversation circles are a welcome variation for discussing experiences, books, movies, current events, social issues, personal problems of living, poetry, experiences, and emotions—among other things. Members of minority groups and less able students are not as threatened in the small circle, especially if it is led by a student, as they are when the teacher leads a discussion and a student must address himself to the total class.

Groupness can be promoted early in the school year, and frequently thereafter, if the students can be involved in putting their common living space in order and making it beautiful—so many classrooms are dismal. Some teachers devote a few minutes to this every day. Before leaving the room, one teacher is accustomed to say to her class, "Put your *house* in order before you go."

Let your pupils tell you what they want to know; and strive to make what you feel you must teach (because it is in the course of study) interesting and relevant to life today. If you do this, students will be more receptive to what you want them to learn. One of the complaints voiced by drop-outs is, "They (the teachers) teach only what they are interested in. They don't care what we want to learn about. They aren't even interested in us."

Even prescribed units can be made relevant and interesting if the teacher is willing to prepare the class for them and to go beyond and outside of the textbook. For example, although Viet Nam affects all of life today in this country and pupils want and need to talk about it as well as about war in general, seventh grade geography classes are likely to begin the year with a study of England because it happens to be the first chapter in a widely used textbook. Asia will not come until the end of the year and then only if the teacher finishes the book. The Middle East is of vital importance, but to approach it by way of a unit on the Hebrews in ancient Mesopotamia is questionable even though that may be what an old course of study suggests. Something about Greece and the struggle there for freedom from tyranny and torture is constantly in the news, yet a senior high school class has to study ancient Greece which the teacher will introduce with an erudite but boring lecture. Some teachers begin a unit on colonial America by showing a popular filmstrip whose second frame is a picture of the Boston Tea Party. One of them, and probably more, let it go by without stopping to connect that historic event with the immediate struggle for civil rights, protest demonstrations, and violence against property which pupils want to and should discuss.

For days before any unit begins, a teacher who wants to tune pupils in, must bring to the room and allow time for pupils to examine and browse in and raise questions about relevant books, magazines, articles, pictures, collections and artifacts—whatever will arouse interest and curiosity.

Instead of insisting that all pupils read certain books because they are on traditional required reading lists, teachers can open the whole world of paperbacks to their students and let the choice of what to read be individual. Instead of using poems just because they were selected by the author of the anthology provided by the textbook committee who probably never saw children exactly like those you teach, let at least some pupils begin to appreciate and understand poetry by learning and singing the lyrics in the songs of protest, of love, of social comment used daily by the popular folk singers.

Open the world of people, places, and things to your pupils.— especially to those who have never gone beyond the treeless and squalid block or tract on which they happen to live. Do this, not only by using direct sensory learning experiences in school, but by taking them out to see, to hear, to examine, to question and to relate to nature, to business and factory, to office and plant, to management and labor, to government, to adults like, and different from, themselves.

Turn yourself on. If you tend to hide your feelings, to wear a "poker face," try to let yourself go. Smile. Express in your face and by your words and in the tone of your voice and inflection and with your actions how you feel about learning, your great interest in the subject you are teaching, your commitment to democracy, and your dedication to education's objective—to every child full and equal opportunity to develop his unknown potential to the fullest extent so that someday he may become what he dreams of becoming.

See your pupils as human beings. Know that they feel and want and need and hope. Try shaking hands with your pupils—especially that one who is disturbed when he comes into your room or with the new one when the secretary brings him to your door or with each one who does a good job of learning. WHY NOT?

Questions to Ask Yourself at the End of the Day and Aids to Use in Planning for Tomorrow

Write down something everybody learned.

Write down something nobody learned.

Write down something different each child learned.

Name the child who knew everything you taught beforehand.

Name the child who learned nothing.

Did you do anything other than mass instruction?

Did you challenge pupils' intellects?

Did anyone work on an independent learning problem?

Did you reject any child?

How many children "failed"?

Did anyone work at the board; did you?

Did pupils do anything other than listen to you, write, read, answer your questions?

Did any child ask a question?

How often did you say, "OK" or "All right"?

Did you repeat every answer?

How often did each child get a chance to talk, ask, tell, answer?

Did any child help another?

Did the class laugh; did you—at someone, something, with someone?

Were you angry—why?

Was any child angry—why?

How many pupils did you praise?

Did you teach reading (not just hear children read)?

Did you teach new words—before or after reading?

Did you read to the class?

How do you feel about the day's work?

12 THE RESPONSIBILITY OF LEADERSHIP

"Only by a continuing quest for knowledge and an awareness of all the shifts and changes that occur in the determining conditions of education can its leaders hope to be responsive to the needs of the individual and of society. Rules-of-thumb and opinions, which too often guide decision making, must be replaced by basic concepts with which to think about the problem."

Ole Sand
"Bases for Decisions," Chapter 2
Association for Supervision and Curriculum Development, *Role of Supervisor and Curriculum Director in a Climate of Change,* Yearbook 1965

How can the administrative staff of a school become unified? The first thing an administrative staff has to achieve, whether it is top echelon or a single faculty, is *groupness.* To secure this everyone concerned must be totally involved for as long, and as often, as necessary in talking about the *kind of school* they want. Discussions must begin with identification of common problems, specification of goals, determination of methods to be used to reach the goals (to solve or relieve the problems), and strive to reach consensus. Then individuals must commit themselves to one-hundred percent implementation of the policies so determined. Participation in that kind of decision-making process creates mutuality of understanding, feelings of personal worth and belongingness, pride in accomplishment, and loyalty to the group.

Subsequent implementation requires group control over individuals and, of great importance, group and personal support for individuals in periods or situations producing doubt, stress and tension.

If in a school district a stated goal of a minimum of a year's growth in skill subjects is set up as a requirement, the staff must know and tell teachers how to discover each child's current level of development in order to determine whether he achieves that much growth. That goal and all that goes with it has also to be implemented through a rating system that is not based on comparisons among unequal individuals and is not competitive.

AFTER DETERMINATIONS OF AIMS, HOW DOES AN ADMINISTRATIVE STAFF MOVE TO ACHIEVE THEM?

The first step is to communicate the goals determined by staff consensus to others: teachers, counselors, parents, and pupils. Every school faculty then has to repeat the discussion process in order to arrive at their consensus as to what kind of school *they* want. To that end, central office administrators must first work with principals so they know how and are in agreement and are ready to allot time for faculty meetings to do this specific job. Principals need support from administration. This is provided through group meetings, conferences with individuals, in statements made to the public through mass media, in addressing service clubs and other organized groups such as PTA's.

The second step takes place in the classrooms. There the teacher must know how (or be helped to learn how) to establish himself as the teacher; how to present his responsibilities and objectives to the pupils; how to give pupils equal time to present their responsibilities and to determine what they are there for. Then pupils and teacher together decide what kind of behavior on both sides will inhibit or further their plans to reach their objectives and fulfill their responsibilities. Thus they set the limits to behavior within which group and personal controls emerge. This is the process which creates groupness in the classroom. Teachers need support from the principal as they strive to do this. He provides it when he addresses the assembly, when he talks to classroom groups, when he is interviewed by pupils, when he deals with individuals who seem unable to live within the limits to behavior, when he meets with individual parents, and when he talks at PTA meetings.

WHAT ARE THE CHARACTERISTICS OF GOOD TEACHING THAT PRINCIPALS MUST LOOK FOR?

Hundreds of articles and books have been written on this subject. Following is a summary of the essential conditions and activities present in, or absent from, a classroom in which the teacher strives to be a "good Teacher."

Emphasis is on *learning* and on *learning to learn* rather than on memorizing the textbook.

Mass instruction is used only when the teacher, with evidence of interest and excitement about the matter, opens up a new subject or presents a new process or an element in the learning process. The total class may also engage at the same time in such activities as listening to music, looking at or listening to interpretation of art, hearing the teacher or a pupil read a poem or story, participating in a trip, listening to a speaker. Those are learning activities rather than instruction as such, and the teacher does not expect or require all pupils to learn the same things from them at the same time.

Individualized learning activities are planned and administered on the basis of pupils' differences in developmental levels and learning styles. Therefore, following mass instruction, small groups and individuals are given learning tasks suited to their needs. If he needs to do so, and he will, the teacher further instructs small groups and/or individuals who move their desks apart from the class and/or into a circle so he can sit with them and in a low voice teach, or reteach, answer questions, and help individuals.

Many sources of information are used in and out of class, and assignments are differentiated in terms of learning styles as well as levels of development.

Able students, once they have mastered a skill or learning task, are used as assistant teachers to work in a one-to-one relationship and to lead small groups.

Able pupils are also given opportunity to meet as a small group for instruction regarding tasks which carry them beyond what others in the class can do and for instruction in leadership skills which they then practice when they act as teacher assistants.

Pupils able to do so receive teacher assistance and the time to develop and work on independent learning projects. These may take them out of the room from time to time.

The classroom decor and equipment reflects whatever learning projects are under way through display of relevant pictures, posters, maps, bulletin boards, and pupils' work.

The teacher makes content relevant to the problems and issues that confront society and to the pupils' own problems of living.

In recitation periods questions are not solely those in the textbook—read from it by the teacher or a pupil. Pupils are not called upon in turn. Pupil answers are not directed to the teacher alone but are spoken so that all can hear. The teacher keeps all involved by asking pupils to express agreement or disagreement, to comment on, to add information. The teacher does not repeat all answers. He praises and evaluates answers avoiding the common excessive use of "OK" and "all right." The teacher does not use distorted questions ending in "what" that call for class answers, encourage guessing, and discourage thought.

In elementary classes there is evidence that pupils are having direct sensory learning experiences in addition to learning to learn from the printed page. Individual learning materials (usually workbooks) are on many levels of difficulty.

Learnings are frequently tested, but tests are used to find out what pupils know and need to know rather than to give marks. Ways of expressing learnings other than in written form or check lists or completion tests are encouraged.

Emphasis is placed on what is *right*. Papers are marked accordingly, and pupils are urged and helped at all times to "get more right." Words rather than symbols are used to evaluate. Marks are not used as threats and punishments. Pupils are not compared with each other or pitted against each other. The teacher shows equal pleasure when *a* child learns regardless of whether it is as much as or the same as what others have learned. Every child keeps a record of what he learns each day. Pupils' written papers are kept by them in individual folders.

Pupils are not seated by sex or race. They know and live within the limits to behavior which they participated in setting up. The size of desk or chair is appropriate to the size of the pupil. Ventilation and lighting are good.

HOW DO YOU IMPROVE TEACHER EFFECTIVENESS?

Provide tape recorders and require teachers to use them while they teach in order to actually hear themselves.

Provide written bulletins, each devoted to a single aspect of effective classroom work, to be used by the teacher as he listens to the tape he made in his room that day.

Provide time, leadership, and consultants for faculty meetings devoted to improvement of instruction.

Provide supervisors, coordinators, or consultants as change agents whose responsibility is to improve classroom instruction. They will have to observe in classrooms; to meet with the teacher observed to discuss methods he used and to plan with him the changes that are required; to return (the next day?) to see what changes have been made; and to continue working with the teacher until change has occurred.

Provide support when mistakes are made. Mistakes must be regarded as learning experiences not failures. Provide praise and recognition. Give teachers a chance to exchange experiences, to help each other, to observe experiments and innovations in the school as well as elsewhere.

RELATED READINGS: BOOKS, ARTICLES IN RECENT PERIODICALS

Learning

BOOKS

ASCD Year Book, *Human Variability and Learning*, Washington, D.C.: NEA, 1961.

Getzels, J. W. and Philip Jackson, *Creativity and Intelligence*, N.Y.: Wiley and Sons, 1962.

Glogan, Lillian and N. Fessel, *The Non-graded Primary School*, N.Y.: Parker Pub. Co., 1967.

Hunt, J. McV., *Intelligence and Experience*, N.Y.: Ronald Pub. Co., 1961.

Keuthe, James L., *The Teaching Learning Process*, N.Y.: Scott Foresman, 1966.

Murphy, Gardner, *Human Potentialities*, N.Y.: Basic Books, 1958.

Murphy, Gardner, *Freeing Intelligence Through Teaching*, N.Y.: Harper and Row, 1961.

National Society for the Study of Education, *Theories of Learning and Instruction*, Chicago Univ. Press, 1963.

Neill, A. S., *Summerhill*, N.Y.: Hart Pub. Co., 1960.

Noar, Gertrude, *The Junior High School, Today and Tomorrow*, 2nd ed., N.J.: Prentice-Hall, 1961.

Noar, Gertrude, *Teaching and Learning the Democratic Way*, N.J.: Prentice-Hall, 1963.

Tanner, Laurel N. and H. C. Lindgren, *Classroom Teaching and Learning*, N.Y.: Harper and Row, 1971.

PERIODICALS

"How Children Learn," Joseph Featherstone, *The New Republic*, Sept. 2, 1967.

"Teaching Children to Think," Joseph Featherstone, *The New Republic*, Sept. 9, 1967.
"The Feelings of Learning," Walcott H. Beatty, *Childhood Education*, Mar. 1969.
"When Learning Comes Easy," Samuel G. Sava, *Saturday Review*, Nov. 16, 1968.

Behavior—Discipline

BOOKS

ASCD Year Book, *Perceiving, Behaving and Becoming*, Washington, D.C.: NEA, 1961.
Berman, Louise, *From Thinking to Behaving*, N.Y.: Teachers College Press, 1967.
Coles, Robert, *Children of Crisis*, N.Y.: Delta, 1964.
Combs, Arthur and Donald Snygg, *Individual Behavior*, N.Y.: Harper and Row, 1959.
Kounin, Jacob S., *Discipline and Group Management In Classrooms*, N.Y.: Holt, Rinehart and Winston, 1970.
Johnson, R. C. and Medinnus, G. R., *Child Psychology: Behavior and Development*, 2nd ed., N.Y.: Wiley, 1970.
———, *Child and Adolescent Psychology: A Book of Readings*, N.Y.: Wiley, 1969.
Noar, Gertrude, *The Teacher and Integration*, Washington, D.C.: NEA, 1966.
Roberts, Joan I., *Scene of the Battle: Group Behavior in Urban Classrooms*, N.Y.: Doubleday and Co., 1970.
Ryan, Kevin, ed., *Don't Smile Until Christmas*, Chicago: Univ. Chicago Press, 1970.

PERIODICALS

"Children and Their Self-concepts," Marshall D. Schecter and P. B. Tempkin, *Childhood Education*, Nov. 1970.
"Clarifying Feelings Through Interaction," Hugh V. Perkins, *Childhood Education*, Mar. 1969.
"Classroom Opportunities to Express Feelings," Mildred Ellisor, *Childhood Education*, Nov. 1970.

"Control and Resistance in a Slum School," Wm. S. Cody, Jr., *Elementary School Journal*, Oct. 1964.

"Dimensions of Classroom Behavior," Medley and Hill, *Educational Leadership*, May 1969.

"Discipline in a Quicksand World," Fred T. Whilhelms, *Arizona Teacher*, Jan. 1968.

"Discipline Means to Teach," Wm. E. Homan, *Sun Times Magazine*, Mar. 16, 1969.

"Disturbed Youngsters in the Classroom," Wm. C. Morse, *Today's Education*, Apr. 1969.

"Helping Children Cope With Feelings," Nicholas Long, *Childhood Education*, Mar. 1969.

"The Emotionally Disturbed Child in the Classroom," Frank M. Hewett, *Harvard Review*, Feb. 1970.

"The Off-Kiltered Kids," M. D. Schecter and P. B. Tempkin, *Childhood Education*, Nov. 1970.

"The Origin of Human Bonds," Selma Frailberg, *Commentary*, Dec. 1967.

"The Way It's Going to Be," Diane Divorky, *Saturday Review*, Feb. 16, 1969.

"Ways of Fighting Vandalism," E. Wade Underwood et al., *Today's Education*, Dec. 1968.

Centers of Learning—The Open Classroom

BOOKS

Association of Childhood Education International, *Alternative Learning Environments*, Feb. 1971.

Kohl, Robert R., *The Open Classroom*, N.Y.: Random House, 1969.

Tanner, Laurel N. and H. C. Lindgren, *Classroom Teaching and Learning*, N.Y.: Harper and Row, 1969.

PERIODICALS

"Corridor Libraries," Helen Grauel, *Today's Education*, Oct. 1968.

"Designing Tomorrow's Schools Today: The Multi-Sensory Experience Center," Henry W. Ray, *Childhood Education*, Feb. 1971.

"Individualized Learning Center," McNeil School, Bowling Green, *Kentucky Schools Journal,* Mar. 1969.

"Individualized Instruction: Resource Centers in Open Laboratories," D. W. Allen, *Classroom Teachers' Association Journal,* Oct. 1965.

"Launching the Open Plan School," *I/D/E/A,* P.O. Box 446, Melbourne, Fla. 32901.

"Learning At Random," Leslie A. Hart, *Saturday Review,* Apr. 19, 1969.

"Learning Centers," *Childhood Education,* 1970.

"Read, Touch and Teach," Terry Borton, *Saturday Review,* Jan. 18, 1969.

"The Open-space Plan in Education," I. Ezra Staples, *Educational Leadership,* Feb. 1971.

"Wider Windows for Elementary Schools," Nathanel R. Dixon, *Childhood Education,* Feb. 1971.

Individualized Instruction—General and in Several Subject Areas

BOOKS

ASCD Year Book, *Individualizing Instruction,* NEA, 1964.

Beggs, David and E. G. Buffie, *Independent Study,* Indiana Univ. Press, 1965.

Bishop, Lloyd K., *Individualizing Educational Systems,* N.Y.: Harper and Row, 1971.

Cutts, Norma and Nicholas Mosely, *Providing for Individual Differences in the Elementary School,* N.J.: Prentice-Hall, 1960.

Howes, Virgil M., *Individualizing of Instruction,* N.Y.: Macmillan, 1970.

National Society for the Study of Education, *Individualizing Instruction,* Chicago: Univ of Chicago Press, 1961.

Thomas, G. and Crescimbeni, J., *Individualizing Instruction in the Elementary School,* N.Y.: Random House, 1967.

Social Studies:

Kenworthy, Leonard S., *Social Studies for the Seventies,* N.Y.: Ginn, 1970.

Jarolimek, John and B. Davis, *Social Studies: Focus on Active Learning,* N.Y.: Macmillan, 1970.

Taba, Hilda, M. Durkin and J. R. Fraenkel, *Teachers Handbook for Elementary Social Studies,* 2nd ed., Mass.: Addison-Wesley, 1971.

Science:

Schmidt, V. E. and N. Rockastle, *Teaching Science with Everyday Things,* N.Y.: McGraw-Hill, 1968.

Renner, J. W. and W. B. Ragan, *Teaching Science in the Elementary School,* N.Y.: Harper and Row, 1968.

Victor, Edward, *Science for the Elementary School,* N.Y.: Macmillan, 1970.

Reading:

Chall, Jeanne, *Learning to Read: The Great Debate,* N.Y.: McGraw-Hill, 1967.

Cohen, S. Alan, *Teach Them All to Read,* N.Y.: Random House, 1970.

Harris, Albert J., *How to Increase Reading Ability,* 5th ed., N.Y.: David McKay, 1970.

Lee, Doris M., *Learning to Read Through Experience,* 2nd ed., N.Y.: R. Vallen, 1969.

PERIODICALS

"Breaking Barriers by Individualizing," Marilyn Jasik, *Childhood Education,* Oct. 1968.

"How You Can Individualize Instruction Right Now," D. W. Allen, *Nation's Schools,* Apr. 1966.

"Improving Independent Study," Jeanette Veatch, *Childhood Education,* Jan. 1967.

"Independent Study As an Instructional Tool," E. Paul Torrance, *Theory into Practice,* Dec. 1966.

"Independent Study at Seven," Mildred Winn, *Childhood Education,* 1970.

"Individualizing Instruction for Self-paced Learning," P. J. Kapfer and G. Swenson, *Clearing House,* Mar. 1968.

"Pupils' and Teachers' Roles in Individualized Instruction," B. J. Wolfson, *Elementary School Journal,* Apr. 1968.

English:

"Communication Skills Through Self Recording," Smith, Adams, Schomer and Willardson, *Today's Education,* Jan. 1971.

"Keys to Standard English," Ron Caselle, *Elementary School Journal,* Nov. 1970.

Science:

"Effectiveness of Individualized Elementary School Science," R. J. O'Toole, *Science Education,* Oct. 1968.

"First Hand Science Experiences," Glen O. Blough, *The Instructor,* Dec. 1968.

"The Living World," *Childhood Education,* Jan. 1971.

Social Studies:

"Black Studies in the Elementary School," William E. Adams, *Journal of Negro Education,* Sept. 1970.

"Ideas for Teaching about Black Americans," *Today's Education,* Jan. 1971, *NEA Center for Human Relations.*

"Individualizing in the Social Studies," J. I. Thomas, *Social Studies,* Feb. 1969.

"Using Classroom Committees to Individualize Social Studies Teaching," L. E. Hock, *High School Journal,* Oct. 1965.

Motivation

BOOKS

ASCD, "Freeing Capacity to Learn" Washington, D.C.: NEA, (611-17322)

Fader, Daniel M. and Elton B. McNeil, *Hooked on Books,* Calif.: Berkeley Pub. Co., 1968.

Kohl, Herbert, *36 Children,* N.Y.: Signet Books, 1968.

Maslow, Abraham, *Motivation and Personality,* N.Y.: David McKay, 1954.

Anxiety in the Elementary School, Sarason, S. B. et. al., N.Y.: Wiley and Sons, 1960.

PERIODICALS

"A Set of Attitudes," Karen Branan, *Saturday Review,* 1970.

"Be Talent Developers," Calvin Taylor, *Today's Education,* Jan. 1968.

"Contact: One Way to Turn Them On," *Senior Scholastic, School Teacher,* Oct. 4, 1968.

"Interpersonal Relations and Motivations," Edgar G. Epps, *Journal of*

Negro Education, Winter 1970.

"Motivation: The Key to Changing Educational Times," Gardner Murphy, *Theory into Practice,* Vol. IX, No. 1, 1970.

Grouping

BOOKS

Franseth, Jane and Rose Koury, *Survey of Research on Grouping,* Gov. Printing Office, 1966.

Getzels, Jacob W., *Creativity and Intelligence,* N.Y.: Wiley and Sons, 1962.

Goldberg, Miriam, et al., *The Effects of Ability Grouping,* N.Y.: Horace-Mann Lincoln Institute of School Experimentation, Teachers College, 1965.

Gordon, Julia W., *Grouping and Human Values, Grouping Children for Instruction, School Life,* June, July, Dec. 1963.

Journal of Social Issues, monograph, *Guidelines for Testing Minority Group Children,* April 1964 (available from Anti-Defamation League).

Haggard, Ernest A., *Social Status and Intelligence,* monograph, Genetic Psychology, 1954.

National Society for the Study of Education, *The Dynamics of Group Instruction,* Chicago Univ. Press, 1959.

Wear, Pat, *What We Have Learned About Grouping,* Education Brief No. 40, HEW, Office of Education, May, 1964.

Yates, Alfred, *Grouping in Education,* N.Y.: Wiley and Sons, 1966.

PERIODICALS

"Grouping," *Association of Childhood Education,* Dec. 1968: "Why Group?", Rand and Taylor; "Some Grouping Practices," Norwin; "Do We Group in an Individualized Program?," Doris M. Lee; "Grouping Through Learning Centers," R. V. Allen.

"Grouping the Gifted," Bruno Bettelheim, *NEA Journal,* Mar. 1965.

"Interclass Grouping for Reading Instruction," Nancy J. Nichols, *Educational Leadership,* Mar. 1969.

"Non-graded Schools," *Education Briefs,* #1, Office of Education, HEW, July 1964.

"The Decision to Fail," Bruno Bettelheim, *School Review,* Winter 1961.

"What Does Ability Grouping Do to the Self-concept?," Maxine Mann, *Childhood Education*, Apr. 1960.

"What Does Research Say About Ability Grouping By Classes?," *Illinois Education Association Journal*, Dec. 1964.

Secondary Education

BOOKS

Alcorn, Marion D., J. S. Kinder and J. R. Schunert, *Better Teaching in Secondary Schools*, N.Y.: Holt, 1970.

Alexander, William M., ed., *The High School of the Future*, Ohio: Charles E. Merrill Pub. Co., 1970.

Bair, Medell and E. G. Woodward, *Team Teaching in Action*, Boston: Houghton Mifflin, 1964.

Gorman, Burton W., *The High School America Needs*, N.Y.: Random House, 1971.

Unruh, Glenys S. and Wm. M. Alexander, *Innovations in Secondary Education*, N.Y.: Holt, Rinehart and Winston, 1970.

PERIODICALS

"How Not to Teach English in High School," Earline Luis, *English Journal*, Oct. 1970.

"Modern Goals of Secondary Education: Individualized Instruction," J. B. Bahner, *Education*, Jan. 1966.

"Team Teaching, The Dangers and the Promise," George Furaro, *Clearing House*, Mar. 1969.

Slow Learners and the Disadvantaged

BOOKS

Carter, Homer L. J. and D. J. McGinnis, *Diagnosis and Treatment of the Disabled Reader*, N.Y.: Macmillan, 1970.

Horn, Thomas D., *Reading for the Disadvantaged*, N.Y.: Harcourt Brace, 1970.

Noar, Gertrude, *What Research Says about Teaching the Disadvantaged,* NEA, 1967.

Weaver, Frank B., *Practical Help in Meeting the Needs of the Slow Learners,* N.Y.: Vantage Press, 1967.

Webster, Staton, ed., *Teaching the Disadvantaged Child,* San Francisco: Chandler, 1966.

PERIODICALS

"Black Dialect: The Basis for an Approach to Reading Instruction," Mary Schneider, *Educational Leadership,* Feb. 1971.

"Dialect Training and Reading," Richard Ristrom, *Research Reading Quarterly,* Summer 1970.

"Effecting Changes in Inner-City Schools," Day, David E. and Louise Y. George, *Journal of Negro Education,* Winter 1970.

"Giving Disadvantaged Negro Children a Reading Start," E. J. Josey, *Negro History Bulletin* No. 29, Apr. 1966.

"Read, Touch and Teach," Terry Borton, *Saturday Review,* Jan. 19, 1969.

"Special Assignments: Creative Arts in the Disadvantaged Elementary School," F. Topper, *School Arts,* Feb. 1967.

"The Role of Teacher Attitude in Educating the Disadvantaged Child," Harold A. Henrickson, *Educational Leadership,* Jan. 1971.

"Tutoring, A Joy and a Challenge," Kinaret S. Jaffe, *Pennsylvania Gazette,* Sept. 1967.

What Children Absorb About Learning

BOOKS

Goodlad, John and M. F. Klein, *Behind the Classroom Door,* Worthington, Ohio: Charles A. Jones Pub. Co., 1970.

Miel, Alice and E. Kiester, Jr., *The Short-changed Children of Suburbia,* N.Y.: Human Relations Press, 1968.

Postman, Neil and Charles Weingartner, *Teaching As A Subversive Activity,* N.Y.: Delacorte Press, 1967.

Schrag, Peter, *Voices in the Classroom,* Boston: Beacon Press, 1965.

Silberman, Charles E., *Crisis in the Classroom,* N.Y.: Random House, 1970.

PERIODICALS

"American Schools: Guild or Factory?," Norman Friedman, *Teachers College Record*, May 1969.
"Is This What the Schools Are For?," Noyes, K. J. and G. L. McAndrew, *Saturday Review*, Dec. 21, 1968.
"Learning At Random," Terry Borton, *Saturday Review*, Apr. 19, 1969.

Marks and Report Cards

BOOKS

ASCD, *Better Than Rating*, NEA, 1970.
Dick, Walter and N. K. Hagerty, *Topics in Measurement: Reliability and Validity*, N.Y.: McGraw-Hill, 1970.
Glasser, William, *Schools Without Failure*, N.Y.: Harper and Row, 1967.
Holt, John, *How Children Fail*, N.Y.: Delta, 1968.
National Society for the Study of Education, *New Roles and New Means*, Chicago: Chicago Univ. Press, 1968.
Saver, Enoch I., *Evaluation and the Work of the Teacher*, Calif.: Wadsworth Pub. Co., 1969.
Summers, Arthur, *Me The Flunkie*, Greenwich, Conn.: Fawcett, 1970.

PERIODICALS

"Child's World of Marks," A. E. Boehm, *NEA Journal*, Jan. 1968.
"Evaluation of Classroom Climate," John Withall, *Childhood Education*, Mar. 1969.
"How Much Can We Boost IQ and Scholastic Achievement?," *Harvard Review*, Spring 1967.
"Individualized Reporting," Esther M. Bearg, *Today's Education*, Feb. 1971.
"I Oppose Testing, Marking, & Grading," John Holt, *Today's Education*, Mar. 1971.
"It's Time for Schools to Abolish the Marking System," Ernest Melby, *Nation's Schools*, May 1966.
"Marking and Report Cards," Louise Saul, N.Y. Times Magazine, N.Y. Times, Nov. 1970.
"Marking and Reporting Pupil Progress," Research Summary, *Today's Education*, Nov. 1970.

"Pass-fail, A System Worth Trying," J. M. Haskiel, *Clearing House,* Nov. 1967.

"Pressures Behind the Grade," Farwell, G. H. et al., *Clearing House,* Dec. 1964.

"Report Card in a Non-graded School," R. B. Chadwick, *National Elementary Principal,* Jan. 1968.

"The Grading Game," Brian McGuire, *Today's Education,* Mar. 1969.

"The Student Evaluation Dilemma," Paul M. Allen, *Today's Education,* Feb. 1969.

"What Do Marks Mean to Your Pupils?," E. F. DeRoche, *Instructor,* May 1964.

"Who's On Top? Columbia Ends Ranking," 90:16, *Senior Scholastic,* Apr. 21, 1967.

"Yale's New System: Abolish Numerical Grades," *School and Society,* 96:61–2, Feb. 3, 1968.

The Role of Leadership

BOOKS

ASCD Year Book, *The Role of The Supervisor and Curriculum Director,* NEA, 1965.

Eye, Glen G. and L. A. Netzer, *School Administrators and Instruction,* Boston: Allyn and Bacon, 1969.

Heald, James E., *Selected Readings on General Supervision,* N.Y.: Macmillan, 1970.

Jarvis, Oscar T. and H. R. Pounds, *Organizing, Supervising and Administering the Elementary School,* N.Y.: Packer Pub. Co., 1969.

Sergiovanni, Thomas J. and R. J. Starratt, *Emerging Patterns of Supervision,* N.Y.: McGraw-Hill, 1971.

PERIODICALS

"Psychological Dimensions in Leadership Development," Russell N. Cassell, *Educational Leadership,* Dec. 1962.

"Revolution or Anarchy in Our Schools," Don H. Parker, *Wisconsin Journal of Education,* Nov. 1970.

"Teacher Morale: Relationship with Selected Factors," Rempel Avorno, and R. R. Bentley, *Journal of Teacher Education,* Winter 1970.

"The Role of Leadership," Keneth Weisbrod, *Educational Leadership,* Dec. 1962.

INDEX